WATER
A PRIMER

Luna B. Leopold

UNIVERSITY OF CALIFORNIA, BERKELEY

W. H. FREEMAN AND COMPANY
San Francisco

Library of Congress Cataloging in Publication Data

Leopold, Luna Bergere, 1915-
 Water; a primer.

 An expansion of the work, A primer on water,
published in 1960, prepared by the author and W. B.
Langbein.
 1. Water. I. Title.
GB671.L139 1974   551.4'8   73-19844
ISBN 0-7167-0264-9
ISBN 0-7167-0263-0 (pbk.)

Printed in the United States of America

10 9 8 7 6 5 4 3

Contents

List of Figures

List of Tables

Preface

This text is an expansion of a manuscript that I wrote some years ago, with the assistance of Walter B. Langbein, for the United States Geological Survey. It was entitled, *A Primer on Water*. That brief pamphlet, although it was widely read, did not deal with some of the topics that presently are important in teaching the elements of hydrology to students who are interested in a variety of environmental problems.

Most books on hydrology are directed principally to professionals—the engineers, meteorologists, foresters, and soil scientists who design or evaluate projects or carry on research. Since in recent years there has been an increased interest in environmental problems, most of which are in some way related to water, there appears to be a need for a text that contains simple but technically sound information written in terms that are understandable to the nonspecialist. An increasing number of courses are being given at colleges and universities under the general heading of environmental science. Such courses must, of necessity, deal with water in some detail; yet few texts are available to cover this aspect of the subject. My own course for undergraduates is typical.

This short book is designed to cover the general principles of hydrology and the facts concerning water use that must precede any consideration of the impact on the environment of man's use of the water resource. The environmental effects of resource use can hardly be understood without some background knowledge of the occurrence and movement of water.

A detailed explanation of the principles that I have attempted to summarize here can be found mainly in the Professional Papers and Water Supply Papers of the United States Geological Survey. To any interested reader who wishes to study in greater depth the subject of hydrology I recommend the publications of this organization.

Luna B. Leopold
September 1973

WATER

PART I

Hydrology

1. Precipitation

WATER CIRCULATES FROM EARTH
TO ATMOSPHERE TO EARTH

In the Middle Ages people believed that the water in rivers flowed magically from the center of the earth. Late in the seventeenth century Edmond Halley, the famous English astronomer, added up the amount of water flowing in rivers to the Mediterranean Sea and found that it is approximately equal to the amount of water falling as rain and snow on the area drained by the rivers. At nearly the same time, the Frenchman Claude Perrault measured the flow of the upper Seine and found it to be only approximately one-sixth of the precipitation computed to fall on the basin. He correctly surmised that losses caused by evaporation and infiltration might account for the difference.

These are the earliest known instances of anyone having correctly reasoned that precipitation feeds lakes, rivers, and springs. This idea was very advanced for the time. Today there are enough river-measuring stations to permit that kind of comparison to be made accurately for many parts of the world.

Water is being exchanged between the earth and the atmosphere all the time. This exchange is accomplished by the heat of the sun and the pull of gravity. Water evaporates from wet ground, from the leaves of growing plants, and from lakes and reservoirs. It is carried in the air as water vapor, a gas. When water vapor condenses it changes from a gas to a liquid and falls as rain, which feeds the rivers and lakes. Rivers carry water to the ocean. Evaporation from land and ocean puts water back in the atmosphere, and this exchange goes on continually: Water goes from earth to atmosphere to earth. The exchange of water between earth and atmosphere is called the hydrologic cycle— *hydro* means having to do with water, *loge* is a Greek word meaning knowledge of. Hydrology is the study or knowledge of water.

CAUSES OF RAIN AND SNOW

A person sitting on a screened porch on a hot summer day sipping an iced drink notices that the outside of the glass gets wet and puts the glass on a coaster to protect the table top. The glass does not leak, so the droplets of water on its outside must have come from the air. The water condenses on the glass from water vapor in the air. When water vapor is a gas mixed with air, it is invisible. The skin can sense the presence of large amounts of water vapor, and when it does the day is said to be "muggy."

The amount of water vapor that the air can carry without loss by condensation depends on the air temperature. The higher the temperature the more vapor the air can carry. When moist air cools sufficiently, there is too much water for the air to hold as vapor. Some vapor changes to liquid water, forming droplets that fall of their weight. The ice in the cold drink cooled the air and condensed the vapor on the outside of the glass. This is the basic process by which rain forms in the atmosphere.

Snow forms by a similar process: The temperature is so low that the water freezes when the vapor condenses. The hoarfrost that forms on the inside of a windowpane on a cold winter day is analogous. The water vapor in the room condenses as ice on the cold windowpane.

What causes the atmosphere to cool so that vapor condenses as rain or snow? The principal cause is the lifting of warm air to higher and cooler altitudes, for reasons that will soon be explained. Around the earth is a layer of air, or atmosphere, that thins from the ground upward. Its pressure is greater at ground level than it is 5 miles above ground level because the layer is 5 miles thicker. When air is lifted up to a level where the layer of atmosphere above it is thinner, it expands because the pressure on it is less. Expansion cools the air by allowing its molecules to spread farther apart, thus reducing the frequency of their collision. Bug bombs and other kinds of metal cans containing compressed gas get cold when the pressure is released and the gas is allowed to escape. The principle is the same with rising water vapor: as it expands upward, it cools.

If cooling is sufficient, the vapor condenses as droplets of water and these droplets form rain. The condensation is helped by the presence of small particles of dust or salt that are ever-present in the air.

The lifting itself comes about in two principal ways. First, winds that blow toward hills or mountains are forced to rise over the obstacle. The rising air cools, as previously explained. This is a common cause of rain and snow in mountainous country. Second, when a mass of warm or light air meets a cold and heavy mass, the lighter air rises over the heavier air. In this situation the cold heavy air acts like the mountain; it is an obstacle over which the warmer air must rise.

There is a third way in which air rises to levels where condensation of moisture may occur. Air close to a warm ground surface is heated from below just as water in a teakettle is heated by the burner on the stove. The heated air expands, becomes lighter, and therefore rises. This is the cause of most late afternoon thunderstorms that occur on hot midsummer days.

Clouds are composed of many droplets of ice or condensed water. The wispy clouds at high levels are composed of small crystals of ice, but dark threatening storm clouds and fleecy ones are made up of water droplets. Why are clouds usually white if they are composed of water droplets? The color depends on how much and what kind of light is reflected from the cloud, and the light reflected from clouds generally is white.

Clouds and rain are closely related by hydrology, and for that reason a brief description of weather processes has been included here. Meteorology, the study of weather, is an earth science, and all the sciences that deal with the earth are closely related to one another.

SOURCES OF MOISTURE IN THE AIR

Rainfall, snowfall, sleet, and hail are collectively known as *precipitation*, a word derived from the Latin—to fall headlong. The word *rainfall* is also sometimes used in the general sense to mean precipitation.

Where does most of the moisture come from that falls from the clouds as rain? Water evaporates from the ground surface, from all open bodies of water, such as lakes and rivers, and, of course, from the ocean.

Plants give up moisture through their leaves. This process is called *transpiration*. For example, an acre of corn gives off to the air approximately 3,000 to 4,000 gallons of water each day. A large oak tree gives off approximately 40,000 gallons per year. This water is first taken up by the roots from the soil, moves up the trunk as sap, and emerges from the plant through thousands of small holes on the under side of every leaf.

Transpiration from plants is one of the important sources of water vapor in the air and often produces more vapor than does evaporation from land surface, lakes, and streams. However, by far the most important source of moisture in the air is evaporation from the oceans, particularly those parts of the ocean that lie in the warm parts of the earth.

For this reason, the rain that falls on cities in the central United States is probably largely composed of particles of water that were evaporated from the ocean near the equator or from the Gulf of Mexico. Only a relatively small part was evaporated or transpired from rivers, lakes, and plants in the vicinity where the rain falls. The winds in the upper air carry moisture long distances from the oceans where evaporation is great.

The heat required to change the water from liquid to vapor in the familiar process known as evaporation has already been described. The air carries away the heat with the vapor, and the heat is given up when the vapor condenses to form clouds. Thus the earth's atmosphere is a vast heat engine powered by the sun. Now the nature of the hydrologic cycle becomes evident: Through the energy provided by the sun, water evaporates from the land and ocean, is carried as vapor in the air, falls somewhere as rain or snow, and returns to the ocean or to the land again to go through the same process.

This universal truth was forgotten in the Dark Ages. The ancients may have had some appreciation of it, for according to the Bible, "All the rivers run into the sea, yet the sea is never full; unto the place from whence the rivers come thither they return again."

As the water circulates over the earth through this grand cycle, usable water is accessible only while it is on the land surface or in the ground.

2. Surface Water and Ground Water

A discussion of water in the air and its precipitation as rain or snow leads logically to that part of the hydrologic cycle that is of most concern to the human population—water on the land. Water on the land surface is visible in lakes, ponds, rivers, and creeks. This is called surface water. What is not seen is the important water that is out of sight—called ground water because it is in the ground. It is convenient to refer to surface and ground water separately in describing where the water is, even though they are not different kinds of water. Both come from precipitation.

PRECIPITATION AS THE SOURCE OF
SURFACE AND GROUND WATER

During a heavy rainfall, water can be seen running over the surface of the ground between blades of grass, between the tilled rows in a cultivated field, or even below the leaf and twig layer of the forest floor. On a steep pavement in a hard rain often can be seen a sheet of water flowing downhill. This "sheet flow" is best seen at night, illuminated by a flashlight or the light of passing automobiles. The sheet flow makes a glimmering reflection. Such surface flow runs downhill to the nearest rill, creek, or gutter drain; and if the sheet flow is visible, the headwater creeks certainly are carrying storm water down to the bigger creeks and rivers. This is the visible part of the hydrologic or water cycle. While rain is falling and the ground is wet, some water is absorbed by the soil.

INFILTRATION

During a heavy rainstorm water may flow down the gutter and the ground gets wet and remains wet or at least damp for days, but during light rains little or no water runs in the gutters and the ground seems dry in minutes after the rain. These observations lead to the conclusion that when rain strikes the ground, part of it sinks into the soil and part runs off the surface to gutters or to natural channels. What happens to each of these parts of the total rainfall will be discussed separately.

The surface of the soil has often been compared to a blotter. Perhaps it could be more accurately compared with a sieve made of a fine screen. If such a sieve is held under the faucet when the water is slowly coming out of the tap, all the water flows through the screen. But if the water flow is increased, the bowl of the sieve fills up and finally overflows because the water cannot flow through the fine holes of the screen fast enough to take care of all the water coming out of the faucet.

If the experiment is performed with another sieve having larger holes in the screen, it is clear that even when the water flow is at a maximum, the screen can pass all the water and none overflows the bowl of the sieve. It can be seen that the rate at which the water can be passed through the screen depends on the size of the holes or openings. Further, the faster the water falls on the screen the larger will be the amount that does not flow through the sieve but overflows the sides instead.

Exactly the same principle applies to rain on the soil surface. In effect, there are many very small holes or spaces between the grains of sand or the particles of dirt on the earth's surface. The soil then acts as a screen or sieve. The larger the particles of dirt, sand, or gravel that make up the ground surface, the larger are the holes or spaces in between and the more the surface acts like the screen with large openings.

When rain falls rapidly on a sandy or gravelly surface, all of it goes through the sievelike openings into the ground. When rain falls rapidly on a clay or fine-grained soil, however, the rate of passage through the smaller soil spaces is less, and the rain that cannot get through the holes flows over the ground in a sheet. This surface part corresponds to the water that overflows the bowl of the sieve when the faucet is flowing strongly.

The process by which water sinks into the soil surface is called *infiltration*. The *filt* in the word *infiltration* also appears in the word *filter*, meaning to pass through. The prefix *in* signifies that the process is one of passing into. Here, water passes into the soil.

The part of the rainfall that does not infiltrate or pass into the soil flows over the surface to a gully or channel and is called surface runoff.

The rate of infiltration depends principally on two factors: the characteristics of the soil material and the type and density of vegetation growing or lying on the soil surface. Sandy soils tend to have higher infiltration rates than fine-grained soils, such as silty or clay loams, because there are larger spaces between the grains. However, even silty loams may have relatively high rates of infiltration if there is a large amount of organic material in the surface horizons.

Infiltration rate is stated in units of inches per hour, the same unit used to describe rate of rainfall. One inch of rain falling on a unit area of ground surface in one hour means that one hour after the beginning of rainfall, the water standing in a tin pan is 1 inch deep, spread across the bottom of the pan. It can be seen that whether the pan is small or large, its depth is still 1 inch, and thus inches per hour is a unit that is independent of area.

Infiltration rate refers to the inches of water that pass into the ground surface per unit of time. If rain falls on the soil's surface at a rate of 1 inch per hour and the infiltration rate is 1/4 inch per hour, the remaining 3/4 inch per hour run off the surface because it has not been infiltrated.

Infiltration rate is higher when the soil is dry than after it is wetted. During a rainstorm, the infiltration rate decreases with the passage of time and finally assumes a uniform and minimum value. The infiltration rate decreases as rainfall continues for two principal reasons. First, wetting the soil causes granules of clay or silt to expand, thus closing some of the pore space between granules. Second, the film of water that surrounds each grain is more or less continuous and forms a three-dimensional network of interconnected veins of water. The liquid flows downward through the net but encounters frictional resistance that increases as the depth of the network increases. This increase of friction with depth of wetting slows the rate of downward movement and thus impedes the rate of entrance of new water from the surface.

During a nonrain period, the drainage of the water out of the soil and the loss to the air by evaporation cause the infiltration rate to change, increasing to its dry-soil value so that when another rain begins, the rate again is high at the beginning and decreases with time.

Normal infiltration rates vary around 1 inch per hour but

may be several inches per hour in well-vegetated areas where there is a layer of duff or organic litter on the soil surface. A typical set of values, measured in a desert-shrub association in southern New Mexico, is given in Table 1. These are average values obtained from many trials in which artificial rain was sprinkled on the soil surface under controlled conditions.

Table 1
Relation of soil texture to infiltration rate

SOIL	INFILTRATION RATE OF WET SOIL (INCHES PER HOUR)
Sandy loam	1.42
Sandy clay loam	1.22
Clay loam	1.07
Clay	0.86

Three infiltration curves (which plot infiltration rate as a function of time) are shown in Figure 1. The shape of the curves indicates that the rate decreases as the rain continues. The figure also shows the effect of vegetative density. The top curve applies to experimental plots 37 percent of whose surface was covered by grass or other plants. The bottom curve applies to plots that were bare of any grass. The vegetated surface, though less than half covered with grass, had an infiltration rate not less than 1.9 inches per hour, whereas the bare plots were infiltrated at a rate of only 0.3 inch per hour.

It is apparent that more of the precipitation will get into the soil if the surface is vegetated and thus less will run off the surface into rills or channels. Vegetation reduces surface runoff and increases the amount of water that potentially could accumulate as stored ground water.

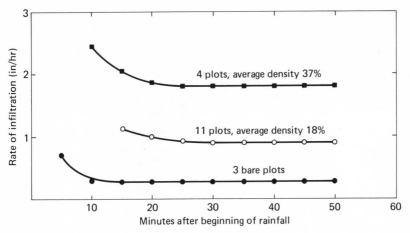

Figure 1

Infiltration rate showing effect of vegetative density. Curves represent averages for 18 experiments on wet soil. Soil is clay loam; vegetation is desert shrub; location is near Roswell, New Mexico. (From Smith and Leopold, "Infiltration Studies in the Pecos River Watershed, New Mexico and Texas," in *Soil Science*, LIII [1942], 195–204.)

Movement of water within the soil

Anyone who has had occasion to dig in the garden soon after a rain probably has found that the soil was wet for several inches down from the surface but dry below that. Two forces, capillarity and gravity, move water downward in the soil.

Moisture moves downward because it is pulled down from below. The pull is rather like that in the wick of a kerosene lamp or a candle. If a piece of dry string is placed so that one end is in a pan of water and the other end hangs over the side with its tip lower than the level of the water in the pan, the water gradually rises up the string, wetting the whole length, and drips off the tip (Fig. 2A). This is an example of the principle of capillary action. A drop of water tends to spread out in a thin film over very small particles such as those in the cloth of the wick or the particles of soil. *Capillarity* is the tendency of a liquid

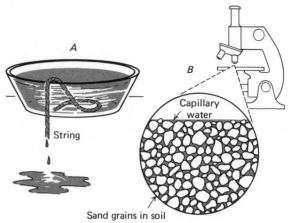

Figure 2
Examples of capillary action. (U.S.G.S.)

to cling to the surface of a solid material, and this tendency may draw the liquid up, against the pull of gravity, as in the case of a candle wick. Similarly, capillarity may draw water downward into the dry soil that is below the wet portion.

Conversely, when the particles of soil are coarse (that is, they consist of large sand grains or small pebbles), water is pulled by gravity and tends to flow downward more or less freely through the holes or spaces. Similarly, water may flow downward through holes made by worms or left by decayed roots.

Consider what happens to moisture in a deep soil. The soil material lying below the land surface is usually filled partly with water and partly with air. When rainfall infiltrates into the soil, it fills the open spaces and temporarily replaces the air. Water in the larger open spaces, like those between coarse sand particles, moves downward more rapidly than the water held in the smaller spaces.

A sandy soil drains rapidly after a heavy rainfall, and after 2 or 3 days only the capillary water is left clinging as a film around the individual soil particles (Fig. 2B). After gravity has drained out the water in the larger openings, capillary moisture remains like the water left in washed clothes after wringing. This capillary water can be removed only by drying. At the surface, evaporation removes the water. Below the surface but in the uppermost layers of the soil, plant roots take up capillary moisture from the soil and thus the soil is dried. When clothes are hung on the line, the air takes up the moisture not removed by wringing.

Unless there is more rain, the soil dries until the plants wilt. When the soil's moisture content is very low, soil particles hold on to the moisture so tightly that the plants can no longer pull water from the soil and they die.

Thus downward movement of water in soil may occur by two different processes. The first is a gradual wetting of small particles in which the moisture is pulled by capillary forces from the wetted grains to dry ones. The second is rapid flow through the larger openings between particles under the influence of gravity, as if the holes or openings were pipes. The capillary water has been pulled downward from grain to grain. The lower limit of this wetting is marked by the change from wetted grains above to dry grains below and can be thought of as a "wetted front" or the bottom part of the wet soil. Further downward movement stops when the wetted front has progressed so far that all the water that has soaked into the soil is held by capillary attraction to the grains; this capillary water can be removed only by drying.

Rain falling on a dry soil does not spread uniformly throughout that soil. It wets a certain depth of soil and then, after the rain ends, the downward movement practically stops. The underlying soil remains relatively dry. To wet the underlying soil, more rain must fall.

AQUIFERS

How deep will water go? To answer this question it is necessary to visualize the nature of the materials making up the near-surface portion of the earth. The earth is like an orange, the skin or rind of which is somewhat different from the inside. The deepest oil wells drilled by man are between 25,000 and 30,000 feet deep, that is, 5 or more miles. This is still an insignificant part of the 4,000 miles to the center of the earth. Yet an oil well, even at that depth, has penetrated far deeper than the ordinary cracks and joints found in the near-surface rocks.

Water moves underground through pores, holes, and cracks that are often seen in surface rocks. Many of these openings result from weathering; that is, from the chemical and physical processes of disintegration brought about by rain, air, frost, and heat. This weathering of rocks close to the earth's surface is somewhat like the rusting that eventually discolors the bumpers of a car or the rims of a bicycle. This rust does not harm the metal underneath but breaks down the surface, develops many small cracks, and causes tiny flakes of metal to loosen from the harder unaltered metal beneath.

The soil in which gardens and trees take root is, in fact, derived from hard rock like that found deeper underground, and is thus like the rusted skin, or flaky brown surface, overlying the hard metal of the car's bumper.

The roadcuts through the hills along a modern highway reveal the change from surface soil to underlying, broken, cracked, and weathered rock. Below the weathered rock is the hard and solid bedrock.

The cracks, seams, and minute spaces between particles of weathered rock become fewer and fewer as depth increases. At some depth these openings are no longer present except infrequently, and the movement of water becomes almost impossible.

There is in rocks, however, another kind of hole that allows the seepage of water to great depths. This is the natural pore space between the grains of the rock itself and differs from the hole discussed previously in that it does not depend on weathering. A common example of rock with natural pore space is sandstone. Many sandstones originated as beach sand on the shore of an ancient ocean. The sand grains later become cemented together to form rock.

Sandstone is one of the principal rocks through which water moves underground. The holes or spaces between the grains of sand permit water to move through the material. When sand becomes cemented by calcium carbonate (lime) or other material to become sandstone, not all the pores between individual grains are filled completely by the cementing material. The cementing material is found mostly where the grains touch. The spaces between grains remain open. For this reason sandstone is generally porous, and not only can water pass through the rock, but an appreciable volume of water is required to saturate it. Other porous materials, such as gravels, were formed in a river bed, then were buried and became part of the bedrock. Such buried gravels may be cemented or may be loose and unconsolidated.

The name for a rock or soil that contains and transmits water and thus is a source for underground water is *aquifer*. *Aqua* means water in Latin, and *fer* comes from a word meaning to carry. An aquifer is an underground zone or layer that is a relatively good source of water. An aquifer may be an underground zone of gravel or sand, a layer of sandstone, a zone of highly shattered or cracked rock, or a layer of cavernous limestone.

To summarize, underground water may move through the pores of rock or soil material, and through cracks or joints of a rock whether or not the rock itself is porous. The cracks and joints are numerous near the surface and less abundant at greater depths in the earth. As for the depth of occurrence of porous rocks, folding and other mountain-building forces during geologic time have caused materials, such as beach sand turned to sandstone, to become buried many thousands of feet in some places. But underneath these aquifers everywhere at some depth is rock that is impermeable and watertight, because cementation and pressure have closed up the pores.

Thus water seeping down from the rain-soaked surface will sink so far but no further, and it collects above the impermeable layer, filling all the pores and cracks of the permeable portions until it overflows into the streams.

Nature of the water table

If water is poured into a dishpan half filled with sand, the water is absorbed in the sand and seeps down through the spaces between sand grains until it comes to the watertight or impermeable bottom of the pan. The sand becomes thoroughly moist before any free water collects at the bottom of the pan. As more water is introduced, the water surface rises gradually until it reaches the surface of the sand.

When there is enough water in the dishpan to saturate the bottom half of the sand, as in Figure 3A, the level of the free water surface can be found by poking a hole in the sand with a finger. This hole is partly filled with water, and the water level in the hole is the same as the level of the free water surface throughout the body of the sand. This level, or surface, is called the *water table*. The water table is the top of the zone of saturation in the porous material.

If a V-shaped channel is made across the surface of the bed of sand in the dishpan that is deep enough to expose the surface of the zone of saturation, water will appear in the channel (Fig. 3B).

Under actual conditions, rain falls on the surface of the ground and wets the soil and rock materials to successively greater depths if the precipitation continues long enough. Underneath this porous surface at some depth, which may be thousands of feet below the surface, there is an impermeable base comparable to the bottom of the dishpan. Above this impermeable base free water has collected, and the top of this zone of free water or saturation is the water table.

The water table rises until it is exposed in the bottom of the deepest notch or depression in the area, which is usually a stream-cut valley. The stream channel, being the deepest part of the valley, corresponds to the notch that was cut in the sand in the dishpan. When the water table is high enough to emerge as a free water surface in the stream channel, the water in the channel flows downstream because the channel slopes. Thus water

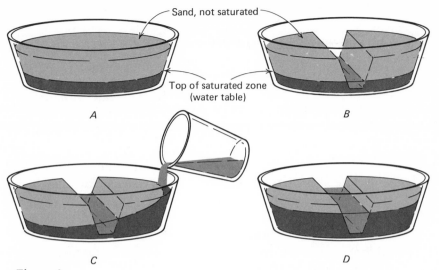

Figure 3
Sand and water in a dishpan demonstrate the relation of the water table to unsaturated soil materials. (U.S.G.S.)

flowing in a river or stream channel long after a rainstorm generally indicates that the water table is high enough to be exposed in the channel. Therefore, the flow of a river or creek during fair weather is commonly derived from water in the saturated zone of the earth material. In a humid climate there is enough precipitation to raise the water table high enough for even the small rivulets and creeks to run water much of the time. In a dry climate the small channels are dry between rains and only the large deeply cut river channels carry water the year long.

Movement of water in saturated materials

This discussion of downward movement of water and the nature of the ground-water table serves as background to a consideration of the movement of water from one place to another in the ground. For example, when the garden hose is emptied of water and disconnected from the faucet after use, it generally has a good deal of water still in it. To empty it, one end of the hose should be held up in the air and the other end should be allowed to discharge water onto the ground. Water is said to seek its own level. In other words, a water surface tends to become flat; water flows downhill, toward the place where the surface is low. By the same reasoning, unless the water surface slopes, water will not move. In the dishpan example of Figure 3A, the water in the saturated portion of the sand will not move anywhere because the surface of the free water is flat. If a pitcher of water is slowly poured into the sand along one edge of the dishpan, as in Figure 3C, this additional water will temporarily make a mound of water in the sand that will force water to flow sideways until all of it is distributed uniformly through the dishpan, as pictured in Figure 3D.

A certain amount of time is required for the mound of water to flatten out and for the general level of the water to be everywhere uniform, because water flows more slowly through the sand than it would as a sheet of water on the surface of the ground. Because of the slow movement of water through the pores, cracks, and minute openings between the grains, the water table in nature is seldom completely flat and horizontal but has in fact an undulating surface. This can be seen in Figure 4A, which depicts a small valley with a single stream channel. The figure shows the sides of a block of land lifted out of its position in the earth's surface.

When rain falls on this area, part of the rain seeps downward to the water table and builds a mound, just as did the water that was poured from the pitcher into the sand at the edge of the dishpan. The water in the ground flows downslope toward the stream channel in a similar manner. If the water table is high enough, the water drains out into the stream channel, as in Figure 4A, in which the water table is exposed in the small stream channel and appears as water in the stream.

As a further illustration of the water table sloping toward the surface stream, Figure 4B is drawn as though the unsaturated surface of the ground had been lifted up to show the water

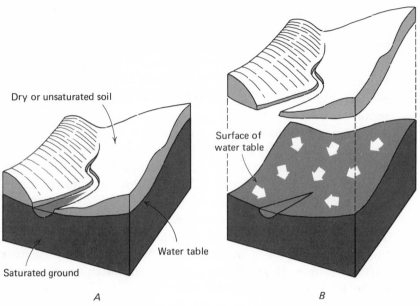

Dry or unsaturated soil

Surface of
water table

Water table

Saturated ground

A   B

Figure 4
Relation of ground surface to water table. A stream channel or rill has water
flowing in it where the channel bottom is at a lower elevation than the
water table. (U.S.G.S.)

table in the block of ground being considered. The following
things that were demonstrated by the dishpan example can be
seen in the figure. First, the underground zone of saturation is
continuous and has a surface that is not flat as long as water is
moving from the high places toward the lowest place. Second,
as indicated by the arrows, water underground flows downhill
in the direction that represents the steepest slope of the water
surface. In Figure 4B, the lowest point on the surface of the water
table is exposed at the stream or river. The stream carries away
all the water that flows to it, even when large amounts of rain
fall and a large mound of ground water builds up. After the rain
has ceased, ground water continues to flow toward the stream
and gradually the mound of water flattens out.

Surface streams and rivers continue to flow for a while during long periods of dry weather, but they get progressively lower and lower as water in the ground is gradually drained away and the water table approaches a flat or horizontal plane, as it quickly did in the dishpan example. Thus when a farmer says that his ever-flowing brook is "spring fed," he is using a popular conception to describe the drainage of ground water into his brook.

During a rainstorm, a stream may be flowing a moderate amount of water. The stream will continue to flow for some time after the rain ceases. However, depending on the size of the stream it will sooner or later dwindle in flow, only to rise again when another rainstorm comes.

Surface streams are intimately related to water in the ground. The terms surface streamflow and underground water apply to the same water. They merely clarify where the water is at a particular time. River water and ground water are the same water, having the same source.

Quantities available from ground sources

A surface stream is not always the sole source of water. Underneath much of the dry ground surface there is a ground-water reservoir from which water may be obtained by drilling a well, as was shown in Figures 3 and 4. The ground-water reservoir might provide a supply of water for future use.

The discussion thus far seems to indicate that a water table can be found at some depth underground at almost any location. This is indeed true, but more information is needed to predict *how much* water can be obtained from the underground reservoir. The differences in absorption that exist underground are simulated by the soils in different flower pots. Some seem to require a whole pitcher of water before the bulk of soil becomes saturated to the top. Others might quickly become so full that water seeps out of the drain hole in the bottom before even a cupful of water has been applied.

The pore spaces, cracks, and joints between different soils in the different flower pots, and also between different rocks in the earth, vary in amount and number. The amount of water that is poured into the flower pot before it runs out the bottom or overflows is some measure of the pore space available for storing water. If a well is drilled into a particular rock that has a great deal of pore space saturated with water, then large amounts of water may be available to the well. But if the rock has only a small amount of pore space, a well may become dry after only a small amount of water is withdrawn. The amount of pore space available is one of two principal factors that determine whether a given rock or soil will be a good source of water for a well. The first is called *specific yield*, meaning the quantity of water that a standard-sized block of such a rock will yield from its cracks and pores.

A rock or soil may have many openings that are filled with water, but if the pores are small or are not connected so that water can flow freely from pore to pore, the rock will not yield all the water it contains. The second factor governing how a rock will act as a source of water is called *permeability*, the quality that determines how readily the pores are able to transmit or allow the water to move. A rock that is a good source of water must contain many pores (it must have a good specific yield), and the pores must be large and connected so the water can flow (it must have permeability).

WELLS

Wells that were dug a century ago were probably dug wells. Well diggers, with shovel, mattock, and spud, put down a hole 5 or 6 feet in diameter and lifted out the dirt by means of a bucket on the end of a rope. When the well was deep enough to reach the water table, or an aquifer, the sides of the hole were strengthened with rock or timbers and the well was complete. Either a pulley was hung over the top or a curb with windlass was built, and buckets were arranged on a rope. When water was needed, the bucket was lowered to the water table, filled, and pulled back up on the rope.

A drilled well is different only in that the hole is put down by means of a bit, which is churned up and down in the hole. Alternatively, a rotary rig is used in which a bit, similar to one used to bore a hole in a piece of wood, is rotated, thus boring itself into the ground. Most modern wells are so constructed that a steel pipe, called the casing, is inserted into the hole, extending the full depth of the well. The casing prevents rocks or dirt that break off the sides of the hole from clogging the opening made by the drilling tool. When the hole has been drilled some distance below the water table, the drilling is stopped and a water pipe is lowered inside the casing. To the lower end of the pipe is attached a screen, or well point, which consists of a length of pipe with many perforations that allow water to enter the pipe but exclude sand or dirt. Water is forced up the pipe by means of a motor-driven pump, or a pump driven by a windmill. Most modern wells that supply water for city or irrigation use are equipped with pumps driven by electricity, gasoline, or fuel oil.

It is interesting to visualize what happens in the vicinity of a well when water is pumped. The pump lifts water out of the hole itself, and thus the water level in the hole is quickly lowered below the general surface of the water table. In the immediate vicinity of the well, water from the pores of the aquifer drains into the hole, lowering the water table near the well. The lowered water table near the well then causes water in pores farther from the well to flow toward the zone near the hole. This occurs on all sides of the well so that the water flows downhill toward the low spot in the water table.

If a finger is pressed into a large inflated balloon, causing the taut rubber to stretch smoothly downward from all sides to the tip of the finger, the shape of the depression made by the finger in the balloon surface resembles a cone. This is exactly the shape of the depressed water surface around the well, and the pumping

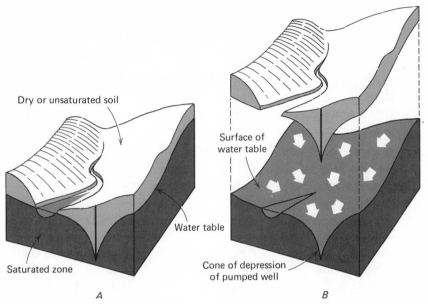

Dry or unsaturated soil

Surface of
water table

Water table

Saturated zone

Cone of depression
of pumped well

A

B

Figure 5
Effect on a water table of pumping a well. (U.S.G.S.)

of the well creates a "cone of depression" in the water table. The cone is pictured in Figure 5A. Figure 5B shows the same cone as it would look if the unsaturated upper part of the block of ground were lifted up, thus exposing the surface of the water table. Arrows in Figure 5B show how the water moves from all directions toward the center of the cone of depression.

As previously mentioned, the rate of movement of water through a porous material like sand depends on the slope of the water surface. When water is pumped rapidly from the well, the cone of depression is deeper and steeper than when the pumping is slow. Pumping, whatever its rate may be, produces a cone of depression that is steep enough to supply water at the rate of pumping if there is enough water in the ground and if it can move fast enough through the pores of the aquifer.

Replenishment of ground storage

Many miles may separate the place where rain seeps into the earth's surface to become ground water from the places where that water might reappear. The simple situation discussed earlier showed that water that falls on a hill might enter the ground and flow toward a stream channel nearby and appear as river flow a short distance from the place where it fell as rain. Water also may flow long distances underground before it appears in a surface stream.

There are large areas where the rocks making up the earth's crust occur in distinct layers, and these layers, or strata, differ characteristically in their ability to transmit water. The earth's crust, as can be seen in many roadside cuts, has been wrinkled, warped, and folded during past geologic ages; rock layers, therefore, seldom lie flat. For this reason it is common for a single bed or layer to be exposed at the surface in one place but extend underground for miles as a sheet. When such a layer is particularly porous (perhaps a layer of sandstone, as shown in Figure 6) and appears at the surface, the surface soil, being derived commonly from weathering of the local rock, will probably be sandy and capable of absorbing rainwater easily. This is called the recharge area of ground-water replenishment.

The area of recharge is indicated at the top of Figure 6. Rain falls on this sandy area, sinks into the ground, and flows downhill. Downhill in the area pictured is down the slope of the permeable sandstone bed or layer, as shown by the arrows. The water is flowing toward the lowest position of the water table, just as in the dishpan experiment. In this example, the sandstone layer gets deeper and deeper below the ground surface as it extends away from the place where the layer was exposed at the surface.

Rain falling on the area underlain by rocks that do not readily absorb water moistens the upper soil layers, but the rest of the water flows to the streams and appears as streamflow. Water

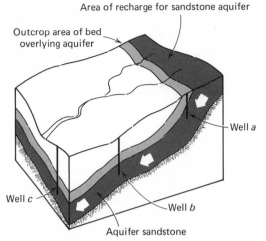

Area of recharge for sandstone aquifer

Outcrop area of bed overlying aquifer

Well a

Well c

Well b

Aquifer sandstone

Figure 6
Relation of recharge area to aquifer. Water-bearing layer, or aquifer, is shown both underground and where it crops out at the earth's surface. (U.S.G.S.)

that wets the soil is returned to the atmosphere by evaporation and transpiration.

The situation pictured in Figure 6 can be found in the Midwest, where the rock strata underlying southern Wisconsin, northern Illinois, and Iowa include some beds composed largely of sandstone. The sandstone is porous and contains large quantities of water—it is an "aquifer." It is exposed at the surface in a broad belt in south-central Wisconsin. To the east, south, and west of this area, the sandstone beds lie deeper and deeper beneath the surface. Many cities and industries get their water from wells drilled down into this aquifer.

In this as in most aquifers, the bulk of the water pumped from wells fell as rain or snow not more than a few miles away—contrary to the old idea that water had to move all the way from the "outcrop" area. The water percolates downward through the overlying strata, which are not as permeable as the sandstone but which are still capable of transmitting water. Where the overlying beds are of very low permeability, more of the water must come from distant sources, usually 20 to 30 miles away. For example, some of the water pumped from the aquifer at Milwaukee, Wisconsin, fell as rain and snow near Oconomowoc, approximately 25 miles west.

How long did it take the water to move that distance? Water moves rather slowly in such rocks under natural conditions— at rates ranging from a few feet per year to a few feet per day. Thus some of the drops of water pumped from a well at Milwaukee may have taken hundreds of years to travel from near Oconomowoc, but others may have entered the ground nearby and may have taken only months or years to get down to the aquifer.

Other extensive aquifers, such as the Dakota sandstone and the St. Peter sandstone, convey water over great distances, but as a rule most aquifers are only of local extent. Many people who own water wells have fanciful notions about the source of water, believing that it "flows in an underground river from the crest of the Appalachian Mountains," or that it taps a "vein of water having its source in northern Canada" or that its source is at the "summit of the Cascade Mountains." Generally they name a cool, wet place of sylvan beauty several hundred miles away. The facts are generally more homely and far easier to understand.

In some areas of the United States, rainfall is so scanty that only occasionally does enough fall to add any appreciable amount to the ground-water table. In some of the arid parts of western United States water is being pumped that fell as rain during the ice age, at least 10,000 years ago.

Water pumped from a well has been stored underground for months, years, or centuries. Whether a well can be pumped forever depends on whether the water withdrawn from storage is being replaced by new water at an equal rate. The situation may be compared to dipping water out of a bathtub. If the faucet is turned off, continued dipping of the water, cup by cup, gradually will lower the level of the water in the tub. If the faucet is turned on so that there is inflow to compensate for withdrawal, then water may be dipped indefinitely and the level will remain approximately the same.

This idea is one of the basic laws of the science of hydrology. When inflow to the storage basin equals outflow or withdrawal, then there is no change in the amount of water in storage. When pumpage and natural drainage from an aquifer proceed at a rate equal to the rate at which rain supplies new water, the ground-water level remains the same. If pumping is accelerated, then the water table falls just as does the water level in the tub when the cup removes water faster than it is supplied by the faucet.

Newspapers have carried many articles about wells going dry during drought years. The wells were being pumped at a rate faster than the rate at which rain was supplying water for replacement. If pumping proceeds too fast for several months or several years, the ground-water level will fall; but if pumping is stopped, sooner or later rainfall will replace the water withdrawn and the water table will return to a level comparable with that existing before pumping began.

It should be kept in mind that water moves so slowly underground that replenishment by rainfall may take months or years. An average pumping rate that does not exceed the rate of replacement of water by precipitation is desirable. However, determination of the average rate of replenishment is usually difficult. If the amount of water in storage is large, the water level may decrease slowly and a long time may be required to determine whether the aquifer is being overpumped.

Returning to the example of the bathtub, if water is dipped out of the tub with a cup but the amount of water emerging from the faucet is unknown, the only indication of whether the water in storage is being depleted is the level of the water in the tub. If water is to be removed only at the rate of replenishment, the rate of dipping should be adjusted until the level of the water in the tub remains constant over time. A decrease in the water level indicates that dipping has proceeded too rapidly.

If three or four persons, each using a different size of cup, dip out of the tub at the same time, while another person turns the handle of the faucet on and off at random, it is obvious that some time will be required to determine whether the rate of removal is greater or less than the rate of replenishment.

A large aquifer is even more difficult to gage. Hundreds of wells may be drawing water from it. The area of recharge, where the rain gets into the aquifer, may be miles away. Rain is heavy one year and light another. Pumping may continue for years before it can be determined that the water supply is large enough to keep all the wells supplied indefinitely. By the time pumping is seen to be excessive, towns have grown, and factories and farms have increased their water requirements. No one wishes to give up his well; so everyone keeps on pumping and the water table gets deeper and deeper.

Pumps are run by electric or other power, and power costs money. The deeper the water table, and hence the wells, the higher the cost of pumping. If the water table falls, the expense of electricity required increases; and if the cost gets too great, the owner finally finds that he is spending as much for pumping water as he would be receiving for his crops or his product. A well need not go dry to become unusable; a falling water table resulting from several years of deficient rainfall or from over-pumping may result in abandonment of the well because of increased cost of power.

Thus it becomes clear why "falling water tables" are discussed with dark forebodings. A fall in the water table is necessary to produce a flow of water to a well. This is the cone of depression about every pumped well. If an aquifer is pumped at rates greater than it is replenished, the water table will continue to fall.

In many areas of the United States, such as parts of the Gila River valley of Arizona and the high plains of northwestern Texas, water levels are progressively decreasing because of overdrafts on the ground-water supply. In other areas, water levels, having once receded to form the cone of depression, are steady and the ground water provides a steady supply of water.

There is little mystery to ground water. Its occurrence and fluctuations have a clear and generally simple explanation.

ARTESIAN CONDITIONS

Ground water under natural pressure is called artesian water. This name comes from the ancient French province of Artesium where, in the days of the Romans, water flowed from some wells and still does. Not all artesian wells flow above the surface of the land, but for a well to be artesian, its water must rise above the aquifer from which the water comes.

An artesian aquifer is shown in Figure 7D. Parts A, B, and C of Figure 7 show, respectively, the flow of blood in the body, of water in a laboratory system, and of water in a municipal supply system. As will be seen, the pressure and flow in a natural artesian system are similar to the pressure and flow in these three examples.

Figure 6 shows a sandstone aquifer coming out to the land surface at and near the top of a hill. Overlying the aquifer and visible on three sides of the block diagram is a virtually water-tight layer of rock, probably clay or shale, that confines the water to the sandstone aquifer wherever the watertight layer lies in contact with the sandstone. Being confined, the water is under pressure. If well b is drilled, water rises in the well and might flow out at the ground surface. Whether it merely rises above the artesian aquifer or whether it flows onto the land depends on the amount of pressure.

The human blood circulation system is comparable to an artesian system. Pressure is maintained by the heart, a pump, and the blood in every artery and vein is under pressure. Friction resulting from the flow of blood against the walls of the arteries and veins reduces the pressure. Thus the pressure at any given

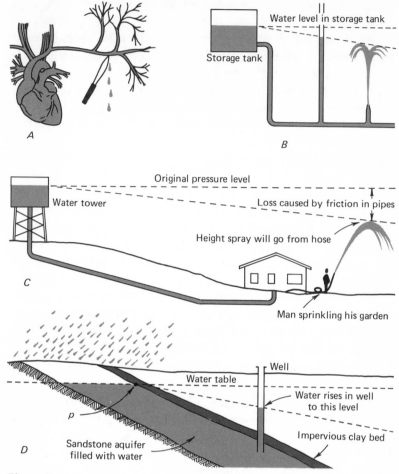

Figure 7
Examples of fluids under pressure: *A*, blood circulation system; *B*, standpipe and distribution system; *C*, city distribution system; *D*, aquifer under artesian pressure.

place in the body is the amount of pressure maintained at the heart less the frictional loss incurred by the blood in reaching any given place. As a result, no matter where a person cuts himself, blood will flow out because some pressure is being maintained at all places. This is shown in Figure 7*A*. If a large artery or vein is cut, blood will gush out because there is less pressure loss in a large pipe than in a network of small pipes.

Figure 7B represents a laboratory system of pipes and faucets connected to a storage tank. Water squirting upward from an open faucet will not rise to the level of the open water in the standpipe because there is some loss of pressure caused by friction in the pipe system.

If a family's home is served by a water system connected to a water tower, as in Figure 7C, the level of the water in the tower is a measure of the total pressure on the water when at rest in the pipe system. But if a member of the family turns the garden hose upward, the stream of water that flows out will not reach so high as the level of the water in the tower. This difference is also caused by the frictional loss of pressure in flowing through the pipe distribution system.

Figure 7D shows in detail an artesian system. Water enters the aquifer through the area lying directly above the water table, or free-water surface. If a well were to be drilled through this free surface into the sandstone aquifer, water would stand in the well at water-table level. Water in the aquifer downslope from point p, the first point of contact of the aquifer with the overlying watertight rocks, is under artesian pressure throughout the entire contact. This water is constantly in motion downslope, but if a well is drilled into the aquifer, as is shown, the water will tend to seek its own level, which is the level of the free-water surface as it is projected by the horizontal dashed line. The water, however, will never reach that projected line because the friction produced by its passage through the aquifer will reduce its artesian pressure. Frictional, or pressure, loss is the measure of the distance between the sloping and the horizontal dashed lines. Compared with Figure 7C, the water table of the aquifer is like the water level in the tower, and the water level in the well corresponds to the highest point the water reaches as it comes from the hose.

3. Surface Runoff and Storage

Precipitation falling on a natural surface can be divided into two principal parts, that which infiltrates the soil and that which moves downhill as flow on the surface. The surface runoff is the part that is left over after infiltration has taken away as much as the porosity and permeability of the ground will allow. Evaporation also removes some, especially from wetted surfaces of plant leaves and stems, from wetted humic material at the surface, and from the surface of wetted grains that are exposed to the air. The evaporated moisture goes into the atmosphere as vapor. Similarly, growing plants are constantly losing water as vapor by transpiration, that is, the emergence of water as vapor from the stomata or minute mouths or holes on the under-surface of green leaves. The combined loss of water to the atmosphere by evaporation and from growing plants is called evapo-transpiration.

THE STORAGE EQUATION

Flow over a surface or in a channel cannot begin until an appreciable depth is attained because the speed or velocity depends on depth as well as gradient and roughness. For example, a bathtub faucet represents the source of inflow and the drain represents the outlet. When the faucet is turned on, water usually does not immediately flow out the drain at a rate equal to the inflow because the drain outlet must be covered with water. If the faucet is opened one-quarter turn, allowing enough water for a person to wash his hands, and if the drain outlet is full open, water accumulates in the tub even though some is constantly draining away. As the depth of water in the tub increases, the rate of outflow increases until finally the outflow rate equals the inflow. The depth of water in the tub gradually becomes stabilized when outflow rate equals inflow from the faucet. This situation will persist almost indefinitely.

When the faucet is closed, inflow ceases. If the depth of the water in the tub is several inches, the water will drain out at a gradually decreasing rate as depth decreases.

Action of water flowing in and out of the bathtub exemplifies the storage equation, which states:

Rate of outflow = rate of inflow ± change of storage.

In other words, if inflow equals outflow, the amount of water in storage is constant. When inflow exceeds outflow, the amount of water in storage is increasing. If the flow of water into the bathtub just described is zero, then the outflow comes only from the stored water and storage decreases at a rate that is directly dependent on outflow.

The principle of the storage equation operates in surface runoff and in channels. It also applies to reservoirs designed to hold water during periods of high flow. (Inflow exceeds outflow and storage increases.) At times of low inflow, the stored water is released. (Outflow exceeds inflow by releasing stored water.) In flood control reservoirs, high inflow is stored, later to be released at acceptable outflow rates.

Channel storage

In a flow system, whether it be the bathtub, the garden hose, or a river, some water must accumulate temporarily in the system before the incoming water flows out at the other end. When a person waters the garden, he turns on the faucet but the water does not immediately flow out of the other end of the hose unless the hose is already full of water. There will be a short period during which the hose becomes full before any water is discharged at the lower end. Similarly, if the faucet is turned off, the water that is in the hose drains out; therefore, the outflow does not stop at the same moment that the inflow ceases.

The amount of water in the hose could be thought of as being stored temporarily in the flow system. So it is with rivers. When tributaries contribute flow to the upper end of a river channel, a certain amount of time is required for that water to appear at the lower end. After the tributary inflow stops, the water that is in transit in the river channel gradually drains out. Therefore, the water in transit, which is called channel storage, is comparable to a reservoir, or the bathtub. Enormous volumes of water are present in the channels during major floods. For ex-

Figure 8
Relation of storage to inflow and outflow: *A*, inflow less than outflow, storage decreases; *B*, inflow greater than outflow, storage increases. (U.S.G.S.)

ample, during the flood of the Ohio River in January 1937, the volume of storage in the channel system was equal to 56 million acre-feet, a volume twice the capacity of Lake Mead, the reservoir behind Hoover Dam on the Colorado River.

Because the river channel system is a form of temporary storage, as is the bathtub, the channel system tends to reduce the height of the flood. As a flood moves down the river system, the temporary storage in the channel reduces the flood peak. The situation is the same as when the faucet is turned on full tilt for a short time but the drain discharges water at a somewhat lower rate because of the temporary storage of water in the tub itself (Fig. 8). Storage tends to make the maximum rate of outflow less than the maximum rate of inflow.

WATER MEASUREMENTS AND WATER DATA

The flow of a river is expressed as volume per unit time. In the United States, this is cubic feet per second (cfs). To visualize this, it is necessary to imagine a trough 1 foot high and 1 foot wide, filled with water flowing toward the end of the trough. Each linear foot along the trough holds 1 cubic foot, or a volume 1 foot long, 1 foot high, and 1 foot wide. If 1 cubic foot of water is to be discharged from the trough every second, the speed or velocity of the water moving along the trough must be 1 foot per second. If can be seen, then, that the rate of discharge is the product of cross-sectional area (width times depth) and velocity (feet per second). The formula for discharge can be written as

$$\text{Discharge} = \text{width} \times \text{depth} \times \text{velocity}$$
$$= \text{area} \times \text{velocity}.$$

Measurement of the rate of discharge or flow of a river thus consists of measuring the cross-sectional area of the flowing water and its mean velocity and then multiplying the two. In practice, the hydrographer uses a *current meter*, which consists of a propeller that is activated by the flowing water, the rate of rotation of which depends on the water velocity. Each time the propeller or vane makes a complete rotation, it closes an electrical circuit that is powered by a pocket battery and makes a click or noise in an earphone. The hydrographer listens to the clicks while he watches a hand-held stop watch and records how many clicks or propeller revolutions he heard during a particular period recorded on his watch. Entering the number of propeller revolutions and number of seconds of time in a table, he reads the water velocity expressed as feet per second.

The current meter is placed in the river at a depth where the average or mean velocity is expected. (This depth is usually 6/10 of the distance from the water surface to the stream bed, inasmuch as the water velocity is greatest at the surface and decreases to zero at the stream bed.) The velocity is clocked in the manner just described for 20 to 30 positions across the river. At each such spot the local velocity is multiplied by the measured depth and by the width of the zone represented by that particular velocity and depth. The resulting product is the discharge in that zone. The zone discharges are added to give the discharge of the whole river.

At low flow the current meter measurement may be made by a hydrographer who wades in the river and holds the current meter on a *wading rod*, a rigid metal post that is held vertically and along which the meter can be positioned to the desired distance above the stream bed. If the water is too deep for wading, the hydrographer mounts a *cable car* supported above the river on a steel cable stretched between supports on either side of the channel. The current meter is lowered from the cable car into the river by means of a winch or reel that unwinds a thin wire rope to which the meter is attached. Under the meter and attached to it is a weight or lead fish that keeps the wire rope stretched and holds the meter in a position directly under the cable. The torpedo-shaped lead weight should be 20 to 30 pounds for rivers of moderate size but should be 50 pounds or more to stabilize the meter in big rivers. Many large rivers are measured from a highway bridge rather than from a cable car. To obtain such measurements, the winch is mounted on a wheeled frame that can be braced against the handrail of the bridge when the current meter and weight are to be lowered over the side.

At the time the discharge measurement is made, the elevation of the water surface is recorded. This is read from a simple gage plate or staff gage, an enamel plate attached firmly to a support. The plate is graduated in hundreds of feet. The reading represents the water elevation at the point where the water surface submerges the plate. This reading is called the *gage height*. The zero reading or gage datum is usually set for convenience; that is, the gage height does not represent the water depth because the zero reading on the gage plate is not at the stream bed elevation. The elevation of the gage datum (zero reading) above mean sea level is often determined by a leveling survey from a nearby bench mark or known elevation.

A continuous record of water surface elevation is kept on a chart in the gaging station. Most people have noticed a round corrugated pipe topped with a roof standing on a bridge or near a river. Inside this structure is a paper-covered drum driven by a clock mechanism. The pen that is drawing an ink record on this chart is activated by a float resting in the water that fills the lower part of the tube or structure. This water comes through a pipe that connects the inside of the gage house to the river, so that wherever the water surface is in the river, the same level is maintained in the gage house. As the river rises or falls, the float inside the gage house rises or falls in unison, and thus the pen records a graph of water surface elevation as it changes with time.

Figure 9 is a photograph of a typical gaging station; Figure 10 is a diagram of the essential features of a gage house. The main elements of the latter are the intake pipes, which equalize the water surface elevation in channel and in gage house, and the float, which is connected to a recorder.

Figure 9
Gaging station on Watts Branch near Rockville, Maryland. The recorder is in the concrete house at the right. The bridge is used to take current meter measurements at high flow. Near the steps (*middle right*), the staff gage is attached to the bridge. Readings of water level on this staff are gage heights. In the channel (*left foreground*) is a low concrete dam constructed to stabilize the relation of gage height to discharge.

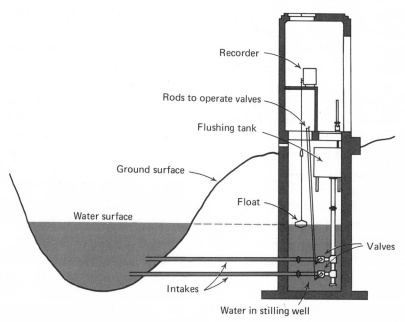

Figure 10
Diagram of a gaging station, showing relation of water in the stilling well to the river. (U.S.G.S.)

The gaging station provides a record of water surface elevation. This record must be translated into flow rate, which, in turn, can be used to compute volume of water. The current meter observations provide the necessary link. By plotting the computed discharge at the time of a current meter measurement against the concurrent gage height (staff gage reading), one point of a *rating curve* is established. The rating curve, or relation of gage height to discharge, is an empirical relation derived from the current meter observations.

Table 2 gives a typical set of data compiled from the current meter measurements obtained at the gaging station on Seneca Creek at Dawsonville, Maryland. Figures 11, 12, and 13 show the measuring reach during low and high flow.

Table 2
Selected data from current meter measurements of Seneca Creek at Dawsonville, Maryland

GAGE HEIGHT (FT)	DISCHARGE (CFS)
9.9	7,300
7.7	2,700
7.3	2,300
6.9	2,100
6.7	1.900
6.1	1,550
5.8	1,450
4.7	1,050
3.3	500
2.8	410
2.7	340
2.5	210
2.3	100
2.1	60
1.95	40
1.90	30

Selected pairs of values of discharge and gage height are also published for the highest peak discharges during each year of record. Often these values do not represent current meter measurements during the flood but are recorded gage heights taken from the continuous record at the gage; the corresponding discharge is read from a previously established rating curve.

Figure 11
Seneca Creek at Dawsonville, Maryland. View is downstream at low flow; bar in middle is composed of gravel. (From *Fluvial processes in geomorphology*, by Leopold, Wolman, and Miller. W. H. Freeman and Company. Copyright © 1964.)

Figure 12
Seneca Creek at Dawsonville, Maryland. View is downstream at flow
approximately half bankfull; note that riffle is drowned out so that no
visible evidence of it appears on the water surface. (From *Fluvial processes in
geomorphology*, by Leopold, Wolman, and Miller. W. H. Freeman and
Company. Copyright © 1964.)

The discharge values for the gaging station record for a given
year are plotted on double logarithmic paper and result in a rating curve similar to that shown in Figure 14. When enough current meter observations are available to establish the relationship
typified by Figure 14, then it is possible to interpolate, that is, to
read the discharge for any given gage height. The gage height

Figure 13
Seneca Creek at Dawsonville, Maryland. View is downstream at a stage
near bankfull.

is read at various hours of the day from the pen trace; these
figures are then entered into the rating curve and the discharge
is read. The discharges may then be averaged to obtain the average flow for the day. This figure is tabulated for each day of the
year and, together with certain other data, is included in a series
published by the United States Geological Survey entitled,
Water Resources Data for Maryland and Delaware, Part 1, *Surface
Water Records*. Each state (or, in the case of some small states,

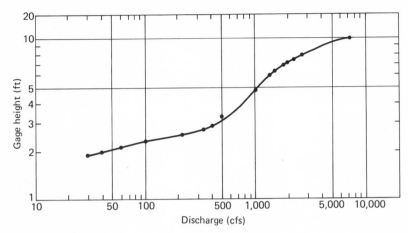

Figure 14
Rating curve for Seneca Creek at Dawsonville, Maryland.

each pair of states) is represented each year in this series, which has been published since 1961.

To reduce the volume of material to be held permanently on library shelves, five-year summaries are published in a more permanent form, the Water Supply Papers of the United States Geological Survey. The summaries have daily discharge values for each of the five years included. These summaries may be found in most large libraries along with other scientific reports of the United States Geological Survey. The report for the period 1961–1965, which contains the Seneca Creek record, is entitled, *Surface Water Supply of the United States, 1961–1965,* Part 1, *North Atlantic Slope Basins,* Vol. 3, *Basins from Maryland to York River.* It is Water Supply Paper 1903. Each such volume contains the number of water supply papers containing similar data for the same geographic area for various years.

A typical set of data for the Seneca Creek gage for the year 1968 is shown in Table 3, which is taken from page 10 of Water Supply Paper 1903. The year used for water data is usually not the calendar year but the water year, October 1–September 30.

Table 3
Potomac River Basin
1-6450. Seneca Creek at Dawsonville, Maryland

Location: Lat 39°07'41", long 77°20'13", on right bank 60 ft downstream from bridge on State Highway 28, 150 ft downstream from mouth of Great Seneca Creek, 1/2 mile east of Dawsonville, Montgomery County, and 5.8 miles upstream from mouth.

Drainage area: 101 sq mi.

Records available: September 1930 to September 1968.

Gage: Water-stage recorder. Concrete control since Mar. 3, 1934. Datum of gage is 214.15 ft above mean sea level, adjustment of 1912. Sept. 26 to Nov. 9, 1930, chain gage and Nov. 10, 1930, to Apr. 6, 1934, water-stage recorder, at highway bridge 60 ft upstream at same datum, Apr. 7, 1934, to June 27, 1967, graphic water-stage recorder at present site and datum.

Average discharge: 38 years, 90.2 cfs.

Extremes: Maximum discharge during year, 1,640 cfs Jan. 14 (gage height, 6.37 ft) minimum, 16 cfs Aug. 28, 29, 30, 31, Sept. 1 (gage height, 1.78 ft).

1930–68: Maximum discharge, 15,000 cfs July 21, 1956 (gage height 12.17 ft), from rating curve extended above 2,700 cfs on basis of contracted-opening and flow-over-road measurement at gage height 9.78 ft; minimum observed, 1.7 cfs Sept. 28, 29, 1930 (gage height, 0.56 ft).

Remarks: Records good. Small diversion at times for irrigation above station. Records of chemical analyses for the water year 1968 are published in Part 2 of this report.

DISCHARGE (CFS) DURING WATER YEAR OCTOBER 1967–SEPTEMBER 1968

DAY	OCT.	NOV.	DEC.	JAN.	FEB.	MAR.	APR.	MAY	JUNE	JULY	AUG.	SEPT.
1	33	35	40	110	99	65	106	65	82	69	26	17
2	32	112	38	100	104	67	89	58	74	76	28	18
3	30	109	340	113	120	69	87	58	80	134	28	18
4	30	56	214	110	96	60	87	61	76	74	27	17
5	28	47	123	90	89	67	92	57	63	61	28	16

	1	2	3	4	5	6	7	8	9	10	11	12
6	28	42	112	80	88	69	82	56	59	56	28	39
7	28	40	117	80	86	65	80	50	54	52	26	29
8	29	39	114	65	84	61	80	50	51	48	43	20
9	30	39	99	65	80	69	78	50	54	48	27	19
10	43	39	188	65	70	76	74	49	56	47	27	381
11	52	37	565	60	65	74	74	48	51	45	37	372
12	35	40	270	55	69	150	71	54	92	43	25	45
13	32	40	163	60	63	332	69	54	134	42	24	32
14	32	39	126	868	61	156	69	49	65	42	24	28
15	32	39	112	482	67	166	71	52	56	41	27	26
16	32	36	99	153	67	214	67	56	153	39	24	24
17	32	39	89	120	65	653	65	54	150	36	40	23
18	78	43	84	110	60	287	65	48	99	35	35	23
19	72	42	80	112	60	198	65	48	82	78	32	22
20	39	39	74	117	65	163	62	52	345	80	48	21
21	36	39	72	114	55	144	63	47	80	40	26	21
22	33	43	89	113	54	131	61	43	67	36	22	21
23	33	48	87	109	59	170	61	54	59	35	21	21
24	32	43	72	104	57	147	80	114	65	32	20	20
25	126	40	69	87	57	120	92	69	78	31	24	20
26	112	39	78	80	56	112	69	52	59	33	19	20
27	48	36	67	90	55	106	66	84	345	30	17	18
28	40	35	206	80	55	106	67	569	672	30	17	18
29	37	33	661	82	60	104	62	270	109	27	17	18
30	36	30	177	94	—	99	64	131	80	26	17	17
31	35	—	134	126	—	96	—	104	—	26	16	—

Table 3—*Continued*

DISCHARGE (CFS) DURING WATER YEAR OCTOBER 1967–SEPTEMBER 1968

	OCT.	NOV.	DEC.	JAN.	FEB.	MAR.	APR.	MAY	JUNE	JULY	AUG.	SEPT.
Total	1,315	1,338	4,759	4,094	2,066	4,396	2,218	2,606	3,490	1,492	820	1,384
Mean	42.4	44.6	154	132	71.2	142	73.9	84.1	116	48.1	26.5	46.1
Max day	126	112	661	868	120	653	106	569	672	134	48	381
Min day	28	30	38	55	54	60	61	43	51	26	16	16
CFSM	.42	.44	1.52	1.31	.71	1.40	.73	.83	1.15	.48	.26	.46
In	.48	.49	1.75	1.51	.76	1.62	.82	.96	1.29	.55	.30	.51

Cal yr 1967: Total 34,261   Mean 93.9   Max 1,830   Min 27   CFSM .93   In 12.62
Wat yr 1968: Total 29,978   Mean 81.9   Max 868   Min 16   CFSM .81   In 11.04

PEAK DISCHARGE (BASE, 1,300 CFS)

DATE	TIME	G.HT.	DISCHARGE
12/29	0200	6.13	1,520
1/14	1900	6.37	1,640
9/10	2315	6.13	1,520

(The water year 1968 begins in October 1967 and ends in September 1968.) The reason for this practice is so that one hydrologic season (that is, the fall and winter, which are generally more alike in weather than are successive years) may be included. The calendar break of January 1, which has no weather or hydrologic meaning, is thus avoided.

A variety of data is published each year for each gaging station. The fact that more than 10,000 gaging stations are operated in the United States by the United States Geological Survey gives some idea of the immense volume of data that is gathered.

In the upper part of the page represented by Table 3 is found a summary of important information about the gage, its location, area drained, and description of the gage. The average discharge, or average annual flow, is the arithmetic mean of the daily flows for the whole record. For example, the 1968 record shows the average flow during each of the 365 days of that water year. The record for Seneca Creek was 38 years long in 1968, so the average discharge, 90.2 cfs, is the average of 13,870 days of record. The highest and lowest discharges of record are given in the paragraph labeled, "Extremes."

The figures in the body of the table represent the average flow during each day of the record for that water year. Below these figures is a series of statistics, each of which applies to an individual month. The "total" is expressed in cfs-days and is the sum of the discharges (cfs) for each day of record. If the month had 31 days, then the total (cfs-days) divided by the number of days (31) gives the average flow for that month; this figure appears opposite the word "mean." The mean daily flow, then, is that discharge which, if constant for the whole month, would give the same volume of water as was actually recorded during the month. Also included in the statistical summary are the flow for the maximum day, the flow for the minimum day, and the mean flow for the month divided by the drainage area, or the cubic feet per second per square mile (cfsm). This last figure is also expressed as another figure, inches of water spread over the whole basin area, which equals the volume of water discharged. The totals and averages for the water year and for the calendar year are also given.

The instantaneous peak discharges recorded during the year are tabulated at the bottom of the table. These are not averages for a day but represent the momentary peaks during storm periods. All peaks greater than a chosen value (1,300 cfs for Seneca Creek) are included.

OVERLAND FLOW

Water that is not infiltrated flows downhill over the ground surface. As water moves over the surface it gradually is collected in the rills or small channels, which join to form larger channels, which also join. The overland flow phase means water is flowing in a shallow sheet. Water flowing through the grass of a suburban lawn is moving as overland flow. Just as in the bathtub, some depth must be built up before downhill movement begins. Measurements made on natural hillslopes under typical rain conditions show that the depths of water in overland flow near the top of a hill are between .001 and .006 foot (approximately 1/16 inch). At a distance of 100 feet downhill from the hillcrest, the depth of the water sheet may be .04 to 0.1 foot (1/4 inch to 1 inch).

Corresponding velocities of downhill flow are .03 foot per second and, at a distance of 100 feet downhill, may be 0.5 foot per second.

Concepts of surface runoff

Water drains from the land through streams that increase in size from small hillside rills to majestic rivers that discharge into the oceans. Each rill, brook, creek, or river receives the water from an area or tract of land surface that slopes down toward the channel. Channels, therefore, occupy the lowest part of the landscape. The ridges of the land surface—that is, the rim separating the land that drains into one stream from the land that drains into another—is called the divide. The area enclosed by the divide is called the drainage area or watershed. The most famous divide is the Continental Divide, which separates the streams that flow toward the Pacific Ocean from those that flow toward the Atlantic (or Gulf of Mexico), but every stream has a divide and a drainage basin.

The drainage area or drainage basin above any particular point refers to the area bounded by watershed divides from which water drains or flows downhill to or past the point in question.

Rills and headwater extensions of small channels do not extend to the watershed divide. All the precipitation falling on the unrilled or unchanneled part of a drainage basin and not infiltrated must flow overland as sheet flow toward the channels or rills. The details of the process of infiltration and overland flow were first explained in the 1930's by the famous engineer Robert E. Horton. His explanation, called the Horton model, was not only widely accepted but was presumed to be general in its applicability. He stated that surface runoff begins as soon as the rate of falling precipitation exceeds the rate of infiltration and after certain initial minor losses have been satisfied. If the intensity of rainfall falls below the infiltration rate any time, surface runoff continues for a short time from the storage represented by the depth of the sheet of flowing water. Another burst of precipitation at an intensity greater than infiltration rate causes another period of surface runoff. His main point was that in a small basin, all parts of the drainage area have essentially similar infiltration rates, and when this rate of infiltration is exceeded by precipitation intensity, all parts of the basin contribute to surface runoff.

Because at any point on an unrilled hillslope, the water moving as overland flow consists of all the water flowing from places uphill or upstream, the depth of flow increases downhill and downstream. In other words, the further a point is downhill, the larger the contributing drainage area, the greater the depth of flow, and the greater the flow quantity.

Thus the Horton model assumes that at times of intense rainfall, all parts of a small drainage area contribute to surface runoff. Indeed, this can be observed in the semiarid western United States where vegetal cover is sparse and infiltration is low. But in forested areas where there is a deep layer of organic litter or duff on the surface, overland or surface flow is not observed, even during the most intense rainfall. All the precipitation apparently is infiltrated. Yet the small rills do discharge water. If water generally is not observed to flow overland, how does water reach the headwater tributary rills or channels?

A group of forest hydrologists of the United States Forest Service and the Tennessee Valley Authority developed an alternative to the Horton model predicated on the assumption that the area within a drainage basin that contributes water as overland or surface flow changes with time. These hydrologists observed that, depending on conditions, only the part of a basin that was very near the channels contributed to surface runoff and the rest of the basin area, further away, made no contribution. This contributing area expanded and contracted, depending on temporal conditions. They therefore called their view the variable source or partial area model. The specific and definitive measurements to prove the validity of this view were furnished by Thomas Dunne, of the University of Washington.

According to the partial area model, there are small areas near the heads of rills and channels that remain relatively moist even between storms. These areas constitute the only part of the total drainage basin that contributes water to the storm hydrograph. When there is a moderate amount of rainfall, these small areas near the rill heads quickly become saturated and the infiltration rate approaches zero. All rainfall in such areas runs off immediately because the local soil is saturated. In many places, swale bottoms at the headwater tips of channels are moist, often even wet, and would infiltrate little or no water if additionally wetted by rain. This is because the local water table is near the surface and capillarity provides water to the near-surface soil. The area of contribution to surface runoff, then, is localized near the upstream tips of the minor channels and rills and along the channel. As rain persists, the percentage of the total basin that contributes to surface runoff increases. The area of contribution can be viewed as a bulb or local zone near the head of every rill, expanding and contracting over time.

In an actual field example, Dunne mapped the area contributing water as direct surface runoff or water that did not sink into the soil. The small extent of this bulb-shaped area relative to the whole hillside area can be seen in Figure 15. Note that the area of the stream channel and its moist edges constitute an important percentage of the total contributing area.

Because a long time is required for subsurface or infiltrated water to move even the short distance to the nearby channel, such water arrives later than the direct runoff and does not contribute to the hydrograph peak. Rather it makes only a modest contribution to the recession limb of the storm hydrograph after the peak has passed and when the flow rate in the channel is decreasing.

The infiltrated water not lost through evaporation or transpiration does recharge the stored ground water, which, moving slowly toward the channel, sustains the low flow of the stream during nonstorm periods.

The variable source concept, which implies that only part of a drainage area contributes water to a storm hydrograph, explains what had earlier been a mystery. In forested areas and other well-vegetated places, water flowing over the surface is never seen. The answer to the previously posed question now seems clear. Only small parts of a basin, those in swales, draws, and low-lying ground near the channel, experience overland or surface flow.

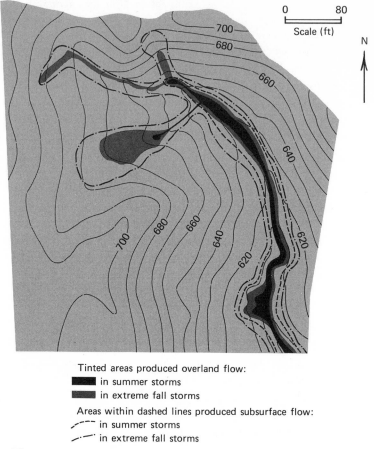

Tinted areas produced overland flow:
▬ in summer storms
▬ in extreme fall storms
Areas within dashed lines produced subsurface flow:
⌐--- in summer storms
⌐·⌐ in extreme fall storms

Figure 15
Areas contributing surface runoff under various storm conditions,
Happy Valley Basin near Danville, Vermont. (From Thomas Dunne,
unpublished Ph.D. thesis, The Johns Hopkins University, 1966.)

THE HYDROGRAPH

The flow of a river is variable through time because the precipitation that feeds the river is variable. During a storm, water is
contributed by rivulets to small creeks and thence to larger
rivers; when the storm is over, the water drains away and dis-

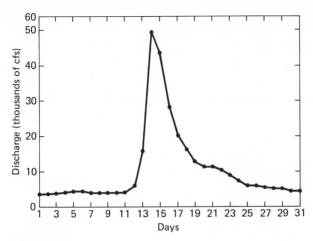

Figure 16
Hydrograph, or plot of discharge as a function of time, for
the Potomac River near Washington, D.C., for January
1963. The data plotted are average flow for each day of
the month.

charge rates return to normal. The hydrologist is concerned with
the time variation of flow.

A plot of discharge rate or flow as a function of time is called
a *hydrograph*. Time may be shown in minutes, hours, days, or
other units, and discharge generally is shown in cubic feet per
second (cfs). Figure 16 is a typical hydrograph showing a rather
simple storm peak. The values plotted are those of the average
flow for each day in January 1963, in the Potomac River near
Washington, D.C. The drainage area above that gage is 11,560
square miles.

The relation of precipitation during a storm to the consequent
hydrograph in a river is simpler for small basins than for large
ones, primarily because rainfall over any large area is not uniform in time or space. A typical relationship between rainfall
over a small area (a few acres up to a square mile) and time is
diagrammed in Figure 17. For illustrative purposes the ordinate
of the graph is shown in inches per hour over the catchment area

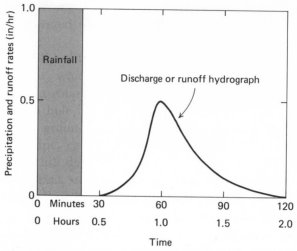

Figure 17
Typical graph of precipitation and discharge in inches
per hour for a drainage basin of 1 square mile
(640 acres).

or drainage basin. This unit applies equally well to rainfall and
to discharge in the stream. To convert the discharge to the usual
cubic feet per second (cfs), the following approximation is applicable:

1 inch/hour from one acre = 1 cfs.

The figure might realistically represent a rainstorm on an
area of 1 square mile. The rainfall lasted 20 minutes (1/3 hour)
and its average intensity was 1 inch per hour. Ordinarily, this
would be considered a short but intense rain: 0.33 inches of
rain fell. The amount of rain is the product of intensity and time,
which is both the area under the curve and the gray area in
Figure 17.

By the same reasoning, the bell-shaped area under the discharge graph also is volume. The area under the hydrograph is
the volume of runoff. The figure has been drawn so that this

area, the volume of runoff, is approximately half the area under the precipitation diagram. In other words, approximately half the rainfall appeared as streamflow and had passed downstream within two hours after the storm began.

If the area to which Figure 17 applies is 1 square mile, then the peak rate of flow shown on the hydrograph is 320 cfs, computed as follows. If 1 inch/hour from 1 acre is 1 cfs, then 0.5 inch/hour from 640 acres (1 square mile) is $640 \times 0.5 = 320$ cfs.

Figure 17 shows that the peak flow at the place where the basin area is 1.0 square mile occurred one hour after the beginning of the rain. This is the correct magnitude for a basin of such size. The figure also shows that the center of mass of the hydrograph lags or follows the center of mass of the rainfall by approximately one hour. Again, this is consistent for a basin of this size.

The storm hydrograph typically has the shape shown in Figure 17. The part preceding the peak flow is called the rising limb; the part following the peak is called the recession limb. The peak or peak flow refers to the moment of highest discharge in the particular storm period.

THE VELOCITY OF WATER IN CHANNELS

The saying that still waters run deep may be a good statement to apply to human nature, but it is not good hydrology. Still waters may be shallow or deep, and deep waters may run slow or fast.

When a river rises, the water moves faster. For example, when the river is low during a dry spell, the water may be moving at an average rate of approximately half a foot a second, or approximately one-third of a mile per hour. But when the river is in flood, its current may be more than 10 feet per second, or approximately 7 miles per hour. At a measuring section of the Potomac River in Chain Bridge gorge near Washington, D.C., during the flood of March 1936, the speed of the water was 22 feet per second, or 15 miles per hour. Speeds of 30 feet per second (20 miles per hour) have been measured elsewhere in natural river channels with current meter by the United States Geological Survey.

At any place, then, as water becomes deeper it tends to flow faster. When it moves downhill, water acts like any other body that is moved by gravity. It would move ever faster, like a ball rolling downhill, were it not held in check by friction against its bed and banks. The speed with which water moves is a balance between gravity and friction. But as the water in any natural stream gets deeper, the area the water rubs against does not substantially increase. For this reason, gravity becomes more important as the river deepens and as the water moves faster.

How does the water speed change along the course of a river from its mountainous source to its mouth? In the upstream part, the mountain brooks appear to rush downhill with a thrust of turbulent white water. They appear to exhibit a high-velocity flow. On the other hand, the large river near the mouth seems to sweep majestically around its bends in a stately, slow motion. But appearances can be deceiving. It is better to rely on a current meter, an instrument designed to measure speed of water flow in rivers.

The current meter tells a different story. The water in the mountain stream on a clear day may be tumbling along at an average rate of approximately 1 foot per second—less than 1 mile per hour. The current in the big river far downstream is 3 or 4 feet per second, and all the creeks and tributaries in between move along at intermediate speeds. Water speed increases further downstream. The difference between appearances and current meter readings is merely a matter of interpretation. Again, the connecting link is depth. At points further downstream, there is more water and both depth and width of the river increase. Therefore, to call a mountain stream a torrent implies that it is flowing rapidly in relation to its *shallow* depth. To say that a big river is sluggish implies that the water is moving slowly relative to its great depth.

In periods of flood, small streams in headwater areas have average water velocities of 5 to 7 feet per second; large rivers, such as the Mississippi, have average water velocities of 7 to 9 feet per second during floods. There is much variation but these are the observed orders of magnitude.

The velocity of water moving downstream influences the tendency for subbasins entering as tributaries along the river not to contribute their share simultaneously. The importance of this staggered contribution in reducing flood peaks is emphasized in the following discussion of the joining of tributaries.

JOINING OF TRIBUTARIES:
EFFECT ON THE HYDROGRAPH

In a drainage basin, tributaries successively join and the main channel gets larger further downstream. Each tributary has a hydrograph describing the relation of discharge to time during a storm event. When a tributary meets or enters another channel, the waters of the two are added but the peaks of their respective hydrographs do not necessarily coincide. One channel may have passed its peak and be in the recession limb at the time the joining channel is still on the rising side of its hydrograph. The effect of the lack of simultaneity of peaks where channels join results in a lower peak than would have occurred if the peaks arrived simultaneously.

An example might help to clarify this statement. Assume that a basin of 60 square miles has three main tributaries, the junctions of which are equal distances apart, as shown in Figure 18A. Let each of the three subbasins or each of the three tributaries drain 10 square miles. The remainder of the whole basin drains into smaller channels that feed directly to the main stream. The three main subbasins thus total 30 square miles or half the area of the main basin at d.

Assume also that during a rainstorm, 1 inch of precipitation was made available for runoff in 4 hours. A larger amount of rain fell during the storm, but the present computation is concerned mainly with "precipitation excess," or that part of the precipitation appearing as runoff in the storm hydrograph. This is the gray area in Figure 18*B*.

The hydrograph labeled I in Figure 18*B* is computed to be the flow at the mouth of the 10 square mile subbasin at *a*. This water must flow down the channel from *a* to *d*, which takes a certain amount of time. During its travel from *a* to *d* it must successively fill the channel and then drain away downstream. The volume of water in the channel in the reach between *a* and *d* acts in the same manner as the water in the bathtub discussed previously or the water in a storage reservoir. The computation of inflow, outflow, and storage for a reach of river is called *flood routing*. Hydrograph I has been routed through successive reaches of channel; the effect of the channel storage can be seen on the routed hydrographs. The first routing represents the change in a routing distance of 2 hours and produced the hydrograph II. That is, for this computation, hydrograph I was considered the inflow graph and II was the computed outflow after traveling downstream a distance equivalent to 2 hours. Hydrographs III and IV were the results of routing 6 hours and 9 hours, respectively.

It can be seen that channel storage, acting as a bathtub or reservoir, decreases the flood peak as the hydrograph moves progressively downstream. The original hydrograph peak at *a* was 1,000 cfs and occurred approximately 5 hours after the beginning of precipitation. By the time the flood wave reached 8 miles downstream, the peak was only 600 cfs, and it occurred 13 hours after the beginning of precipitation.

If the storm had covered all of the 60-square-mile basin, the hydrographs for each of the three subbasins would have been the same. But because the subbasins are at different distances above *d*, the water from the nearest one entering at *c* would already have drained partly away by the time the contribution from the farther ones, *b* and *a*, arrived at *d*.

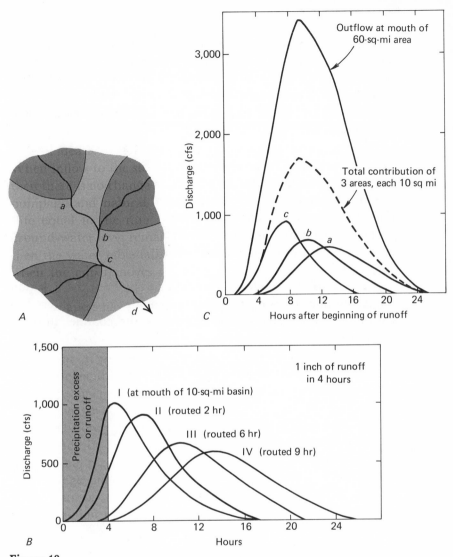

Figure 18
Basin map and hydrographs of subbasins in a drainage area of 60 square
miles. The basin with its subbasins is shown in Figure 18A. Figure 18B shows
the hydrograph from subbasin a at the mouth and routed 2, 6, and 9 hours.
The addition of hydrographs of subbasins a, b, and c is shown in Figure 18C.
(After Leopold and Maddock, *The flood control controversy.* New York:
Ronald Press, 1954.)

This difference in distance determines both the timing and peak at the time the hydrographs of various tributaries pass a downstream point. Figure 18C shows the contributions from subbasins c, b, and a at point d. The hydrograph from a, having been routed the farthest, is later and has a lower peak than the hydrographs from b or c.

When the three hydrographs, c, b, and a, as they pass point d are added, the sum is the dashed graph. But a, b, and c are only half of the area upstream of point d, so the remaining half is assumed to have a similar contribution. The computed hydrograph from the whole of the 60 square miles has been shown as the largest solid line graph in Figure 18C and represents twice or double the dashed-line graph from the three contributing subbasins.

The downstream hydrograph is thus built from the addition of contributions from upstream areas, each routed or altered as a result of the storage in the volume of the channel through which it flows.

4. The Drainage Network

Small creeks join to form larger streams. These have as tributaries small creeks and finally join a river of equal or larger size. Large rivers are formed by the joining of ones of intermediate size.

The pattern of this joining is much like the branching of trees. Surprisingly, however, this successive merging is highly organized and is one of the many aspects of dynamic equilibrium that is maintained within the river system.

The high degree of organization may be illustrated by a network analysis, one of the several important contributions of Robert E. Horton. Let the size of a river be designated by its order, here defined. A stream of first order is one that has no tributaries.

When two streams of first order join, a stream segment of second order begins that may have one or several first-order tributaries along its length. However, when two streams of second order join, there the second-order segments end and the single stream of third order begins. This stream extends until joined by another third-order river, and there the fourth order begins.

In simple terms, the stream network can be approximated by those channels colored blue, either solid or with dashed lines, on the topographic maps of the United States Geological Survey. The simplest way to make a network analysis is to place a piece of tracing paper over the topographic sheets and trace all the blue lines, thus eliminating the many other features shown on the topographic quadrangle. The traced net can then be analyzed by the rules given previously, each stream segment to be colored with a color indicating a different order number.

Figure 19 shows the network for part of the drainage basin of Seneca Creek. The basin of 100 square miles above Dawsonville, used as the example for several demonstrations in this book, was too large for easy presentation. One of the main branches, Little Seneca Creek, is shown on the network map.

After the order numbers have been assigned, the length of each segment can be measured with a scale and then recorded both in a tabulation and beside the respective segments on the map. The number and mean length of the segments of each order can then be computed.

This set of rules for stream orders is an adaptation of the original suggestion made by Horton. It was devised by A. N. Strahler and is widely used because of its simplicity.

Table 4 presents the average lengths of various orders for the two main branches of Seneca Creek that meet just upstream from the gaging station at Dawsonville, Maryland.

When such data are plotted on semilogarithmic paper, the nature of the geometric progression becomes clear. The data for Seneca Creek above Dawsonville are plotted in Figure 20. Note

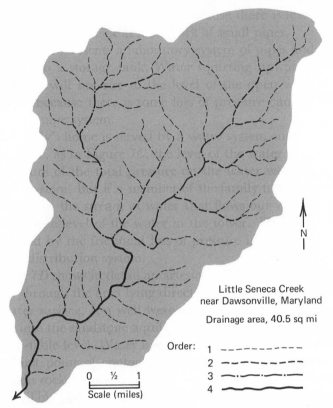

Figure 19
Channel network of Little Seneca Creek above Dawsonville, Maryland. Different stream orders are indicated by different symbols.

the tendency for straight-line plots. As the drainage basin size increases, the variability is diminished and the plots are more nearly straight. As shown in this example, even in a basin of 100 square miles, the average length of first-order streams is aberrant, for it is large relative to the lengths for streams of higher order.

Table 4
**Stream network analysis: Number and average lengths of
channels of different order**

ORDER	LITTLE SENECA CREEK		GREAT SENECA CREEK		TOTAL ABOVE GAGING STATION AT DAWSONVILLE, MARYLAND	
	NUMBER OF STREAMS	AVERAGE LENGTH (MILES)	NUMBER OF STREAMS	AVERAGE LENGTH (MILES)	NUMBER OF STREAMS	AVERAGE LENGTH (MILES)
1	62	.87	103	.59	165	.73
2	12	.91	24	.78	36	.83
3	3	3.85	5	1.64	8	2.74
4	1	5.38	1	10.6	2	7.95

The consistency of such geometric relations as number, length, and order is indicative of the highly organized character of river systems. The slope of the line shows number of streams as function of order; a straight line indicates a constant ratio of the number of streams of a given order to the number of streams of next higher order. In the plot for Seneca Creek, there are 4.6 times as many first-order streams as second-order streams. This is the usual magnitude of this ratio for most rivers. It means that when a sketch of a stream net is drawn, 4 or 5 tributaries should be drawn to any segment of a given order. The usual number for river systems is between 3.5 and 4.5.

The reasons why channel networks are constructed in this particular way are related to a central tendency for such open systems to be in quasi-equilibrium. These systems tend to minimize the total energy expenditure; in other words, they tend toward a certain efficiency. For example, a principal purpose of the branching pattern of a tree is to hold up the leaves to the sun. There are several alternative patterns of branch attachment

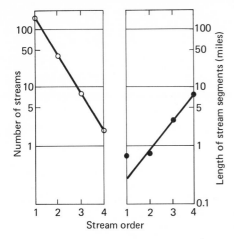

Figure 20
Plot of average stream length and number of streams as functions of stream order (Strahler order). The basin is Seneca Creek above Dawsonville, Maryland, drainage area 100 square miles.

to the central trunk. The pattern most frequently observed in Nature is one that tends to minimize the total length of the branches on a tree.

The ratio of the number and lengths of branches of various orders is approximately comparable in trees and in river systems. This pattern tends to minimize total length and closely approximates the most probable network that would result from entirely random joining. Thus branching patterns of trees, rivers, blood vessels in animal tissue, and other natural networks are not only similar, but are designed for efficiency and stability.

5. Flow Frequency and Floods

TABULATION OF PEAK DISCHARGES

Table 5 lists flood discharges with dates and corresponding gage heights measured at the gaging station of Seneca Creek at Dawsonville, Maryland. Such tables are published for nearly every gaging station in the United States in a most useful set of volumes within the series of Water Supply Papers of the United States Geological Survey. The volumes pertaining to this subject are entitled, *Magnitude and Frequency of Floods in the United States.* The subtitle of each volume indicates which river basins are included. The data for Seneca Creek given in Table 5 appear in Water Supply Paper 1672.

69

Table 5
Peak stages and discharges
6450. Seneca Creek at Dawsonville, Maryland

Location: Lat 39°07'41", long 77°20'13", on right bank 60 ft downstream from bridge on State Highway 28, 150 ft downstream from mouth of Great Seneca Creek, and 1/2 mile east of Dawsonville, Montgomery County.

Drainage area: 101 sq mi.

Gage: Nonrecording prior to Nov. 10, 1930; recording thereafter. At site 60 ft upstream prior to Apr. 7, 1934. Datum of gage is 214.15 ft above mean sea level, adjustment of 1912.

Stage-discharge relation: Defined by current-meter measurements below 2,700 cfs and extended above on basis of contracted-opening and flow-over-road measurement at 7,330 cfs.

WATER YEAR	DATE	GAGE HEIGHT (FEET)	DISCHARGE (CFS)
1931	June 16, 1931	5.28	1,440
	July 1, 1931	6.08	1,730
1932	Mar. 28, 1932	5.56	1,380
1933	Oct. 18, 1932	6.59	1,730
	Nov. 1, 1932	6.80	1,880
	May 27, 1933	6.73	1,840
	July 3, 1933	8.20	3,300
	Aug. 24, 1933	10.30	9,300
1934	Mar. 3, 1934	7.30	2,310
	Sept. 17, 1934	7.30	2,410
1935	May 7, 1935	6.10	1,420
1936	Jan. 3, 1936	6.88	2,020
	Feb. 14, 1936	7.42[a]	1,300
	Feb. 26, 1936	6.33	1,580
	Aug. 29, 1936	5.55	1,350
1937	Apr. 26, 1937	6.78	2,030
	June 4, 1937	5.68	1,370
	June 18, 1937	7.40	2,560
	Aug. 23, 1937	6.27	1,680
	Aug. 27, 1937	7.45	2,610
1938	Oct. 23, 1937	7.08	2,280
	Oct. 28, 1937	6.57	1,840
	Nov. 13, 1937	6.87	2,070

(Continued)

Table 5—*Continued*

WATER YEAR	DATE	GAGE HEIGHT (FEET)	DISCHARGE (CFS)
1939	Jan. 30, 1939	6.93	2,150
	Feb. 3, 1939	5.81	1,420
	June 23, 1939	5.57	1,320
1940	Apr. 9, 1940	5.41	1,250
	Apr. 20, 1940	6.41	1,740
	July 24, 1940	5.40	1,250
1941	June 23, 1941	5.50	1,300
1942	May 22, 1942	5.86	1,460
	Sept. 27, 1942	5.83	1,410
1943	Oct. 14, 1942	6.03	1,510
	Oct. 16, 1942	8.31	3,620
	Oct. 26, 1942	6.14	1,560
	Dec. 30, 1942	6.74	1,990
1944	Nov. 9, 1943	7.52	2,660
	Dec. 26, 1943	5.78	1,410
	Jan. 4, 1944	7.12	2,280
1945	Jan. 1, 1945	5.72	1,370
	June 21, 1945	6.02	1,510
	Aug. 1, 1945	6.90	2,110
1946	Nov. 28, 1945	—	1,550[b]
	Dec. 6, 1945	6.52	1,810
	May 18, 1945	5.83	1,410
	May 21, 1946	7.07	2,240
	June 2, 1946	7.73	2,940
	Sept. 23, 1946	6.30	1,680
1947	Aug. 20, 1947	6.75	1,990
1948	Jan. 1, 1948	5.67	1,350
	Feb. 14, 1948	6.70	1,950
	June 30, 1948	6.78	1,990
1949	Nov. 29, 1948	5.99	1,510
	Dec. 4, 1948	6.52	1,810
	Dec. 30, 1948	6.87	2,070
	Jan. 5, 1949	6.85	2,070
	July 16, 1949	7.03	2,240
1950	Mar. 23, 1950	7.12	2,280
	July 15, 1950	6.60	1,880

Table 5—*Continued*

WATER YEAR	DATE	GAGE HEIGHT (FEET)	DISCHARGE (CFS)
1951	Nov. 25, 1950	—	1,990[b]
	Dec. 4, 1950	7.26	2,420
	Feb. 7, 1951	6.98	2,190
	June 4, 1951	7.21	2,370
	June 10, 1951	7.02	2,190
	June 13, 1951	6.26	1,650
	July 28, 1951	5.85	1,440
1952	Apr. 27, 1952	7.17	21,90
	May 26, 1952	5.94	1,440
	June 10, 1952	7.02	2,070
	Aug. 20, 1952	7.08	2,110
	Sept. 1, 1952	7.77	2,810
1953	Nov. 22, 1952	9.78	7,330
	Mar. 15, 1953	6.25	1,580
	Mar. 24, 1953	6.07	1,490
	Mar. 26, 1953	7.56	2,580
	Mar. 31, 1953	6.05	1,480
	Aug. 9, 1953	8.01	3,110
1954	Dec. 14, 1953	5.45	1,240
1955	Feb. 7, 1955	6.10	1,500
	Aug. 13, 1955	7.60	2,620
1956	Mar. 14, 1956	6.05	1,480
	July 5, 1956	6.59	1,760
	July 21, 1956	12.17	15,000
1957	Apr. 5, 1957	4.54	959
1958	Dec. 21, 1957	8.35	3,640
	Dec. 26, 1957	6.40	1,650
	Jan. 14, 1958	7.22	2,240
	Jan. 25, 1958	6.12	1,510
1959	Aug. 8, 1959	6.90	1,970
1960	Feb. 19, 1960	6.30	1,600
1961	Apr. 13, 1961	6.71	1,840
	June 10, 1961	7.98	3,070
	June 14, 1961	6.01	1,460

[a]Backwater from ice.
[b]Estimated.

For each gaging station a base figure or lowest figure is chosen that is appropriate to the size of the basin. For this station, the base is 1,300 cfs, meaning that the table includes all momentary peak discharges higher than that base figure.

The words "partial-duration series" mean that all flood peaks are tabulated, not merely the single highest peak in each year of record. The latter series of annual peaks is discussed in the next section, headed "Flood Frequency."

The channel of Seneca Creek at the station has a capacity of approximately 1,550 cfs without overflow. This is the *bankfull discharge*. Its determination will be discussed later. Many peak discharges are higher than that figure, and of course many may be lower. A count of the number of peak events in Table 5 that are equal to or that exceed bankfull, 1,550 cfs, gives a figure of 61 events in the period 1931–1961. This means that there were, on the average, 2 flows per year that were equal to or greater than bankfull. A figure of 2 flows per year is the approximate average for most rivers.

FLOOD FREQUENCY

All rivers naturally experience high discharge at a time of heavy precipitation. Fluctuation of flow with time is a consequence of the sequence of stormy periods and nonstorm periods.

The river cannot form a channel that would convey without overflow all possible flow events. In fact, the channel can contain within its banks only a discharge of modest size. The greater discharges must overflow the valley floor within which the channel occurs. For this reason the flat valley floor or flood plain is indeed part of the channel during unusual storm events. When man uses this part of the river by constructing buildings or roads or by growing crops there, he is encroaching on the river and his efforts may be damaged or destroyed when overflow occurs.

Floods, then, are events of such magnitude that the channel cannot accommodate the peak discharge. A flood is a flow in excess of channel capacity. It is a normal and expected characteristic of rivers.

Floods, or flows in excess of bankfull, are relatively common. Most rivers, on the average, experience discharges in excess of bankfull capacity approximately 2 or 3 times a year.

Floods are significant climatically controlled events. The occurrence of floods is studied as a probability problem, and knowledge of the probability of flood occurrence is needed for a variety of engineering and economic reasons. These needs and potential uses have led to a considerable effort over many years to develop systematic procedures for analyzing flood probability. Probability studies of flood occurrence are also important tools in geomorphology.

In contrast with records of annual or monthly value of mean runoff, flood occurrences may be treated as random events, for the meteorologic and hydrologic factors affecting flood production do vary with time sufficiently that the combinations have many characteristics of chance events. The underlying premise is that the floods occurring during a specific period constitute a sample of an indefinitely large population in time. For example, if the largest flood recorded in a 30-year period was of a certain size, a flood of equal magnitude will probably occur during the next 30 years.

Several relatively simple procedures are used for computing flood frequency. One of the most practical begins with the tabulation of the highest discharge in each year of record at the station. Momentary peak discharges are used for this array if they are available. The sample then includes only one event in each year. The mean of this series is called the *mean annual flood*.

The plotting position for individual items in the array is determined by the formula

$$\text{Recurrence interval} = \frac{N + 1}{M},$$

where N equals the number of years of record and M is the rank of the individual item in the array.

The ordinate scale, discharge in cfs, may be either arithmetic or logarithmic. The abscissa is recurrence interval in years. In the usual array or annual flood series, the peak discharge for each year is included. It is the *annual flood* in the sense that it is the highest of *all* flood events in that year. When these annual events are plotted against the recurrence interval, the interpretation of the plot is as follows: It is probable that, on the average over a period of years, the recurrence interval of an annual peak of Y cfs will be X years. The mode of plotting and the use of such a graph can be explained by an example.

From the published data the highest discharge in each year of record between 1928 and 1958 has been determined; these figures are compiled in Table 6.

Column 3 of the table shows the rank order of the discharge values. The largest discharge occurred in 1956 and has the rank of 1. The second largest was in 1933 and has the rank of 2.

The recurrence interval appears in the fourth column and is computed using the quantity

$$N + 1/M.$$

In the 31-year record, $N + 1$ is 32. For the highest flood, rank 1, the recurrence interval is $32/1 = 32$. On the frequency graph, Figure 21, the recurrence interval of 32 on the abscissa is plotted against a discharge of 15,000 cfs on the ordinate. The second-ranking flow, 9,300 cfs, is plotted against $32/2 = 16$ years.

The use of a logarithmic scale for the ordinate tends to make the plotted graph more or less straight, but a completely straight line is neither expected or common.

The largest flood or several floods frequently deviate markedly from the trend established by the remainder of the array (see Fig. 21). This can be interpreted in two ways. First, it could be said that the three largest floods on Seneca Creek during the period of record are larger than the floods that would be expected in successive samples of 31 years. In other words, during the particular 31-year period, several floods were larger than would be expected on the average in that length of record. Using

Table 6
Peak discharges for each year of record, 1928-1958,
for Seneca Creek at Dawsonville, Maryland,
including rank order and plotting position

ANNUAL PEAK FLOWS		RANK ORDER	RECURRENCE INTERVAL (YRS) $\dfrac{N+1}{M}$
YEAR	DISCHARGE (CFS)		
1928	3,800	4	8.00
1929	1,600	24	1.33
1930	1,450	26	1.23
1931	1,730	23	1.39
1932	1,380	28	1.14
1933	9,300	2	16.0
1934	2,410	13	2.46
1935	1,420	27	1.19
1936	2,020	19	1.68
1937	2,610	11	2.91
1938	2,280	14	2.29
1939	2,150	17	1.88
1940	1,740	22	1.45
1941	1,300	29	1.10
1942	1,460	25	1.28
1943	3,620	6	5.33
1944	2,660	9	3.56
1945	2,110	18	1.78
1946	2,940	7	4.57
1947	1,990	20	1.60
1948	1,990	21	1.52
1949	2,240	16	2.00
1950	2,280	15	2.13
1951	2,420	12	2.67
1952	2,810	8	4.00
1953	7,330	3	10.70
1954	1,240	30	1.07
1955	2,620	10	3.20
1956	15,000	1	32.00
1957	959	31	1.03
1958	3,640	5	6.40

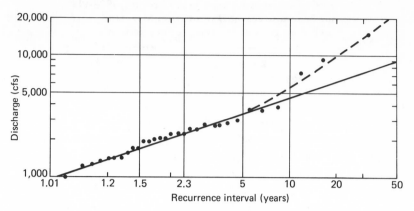

Figure 21
Flood frequency graph, Seneca Creek at Dawsonville, Maryland. The data represent the highest peak discharge in each year of record and appear in Table 6.

this interpretation, an almost straight line or smooth curve might be drawn through all the rest of the points and the largest three floods would then be off the curve. This interpretation is shown by the solid line. The second highest discharge, 9,300 cfs, would have an expected recurrence interval read off the extended straight line of approximately 50 years. The highest would be even less frequent.

Alternatively, a smooth curve of best fit could be drawn for all the points as represented by the dashed line drawn on Figure 21. According to this interpretation the highest flood would have an expected recurrence interval of 32 years and the second highest would be approximately 20 years.

These differences are emphasized here to show that in many hydrologic records that are short, it is not really known what a much longer record would show. Thus the probable recurrence interval of any of the highest flows in such a short record can be stated only within certain limits; there is no single or assured answer.

This difficulty is partly overcome by using the average for many gaging stations in a region, the result of which is a regional flood frequency curve. Because different gaging stations have different drainage areas and thus produce different magnitudes of flood peak for a rainstorm of a given size, it is necessary to reduce the records to a common base that takes out the effect of drainage basin size. This is done by expressing the discharge values as ratios to the mean annual flood.

The mean annual flood is the arithmetic mean of the annual flood peaks, or the mean of values in column 2 of Table 6. Each annual flood figure in cubic feet per second is divided by the mean annual flood and the quotient is plotted against the recurrence interval. A typical plot of "ratio to mean annual flood" versus "recurrence interval" is shown on page 9 of Water Supply Paper 1672, which is applicable to the region that includes Seneca Creek at Dawsonville, Maryland.

Mathematical analysis has shown that the mean annual flood has, on the average, a recurrence interval of 2.3 years; that is, once every 2.3 years on the average, the highest flow of the year will equal or exceed the value of the mean annual flood.

THE BANKFULL DISCHARGE

As discussed earlier, the channel will pass without overflow a moderate discharge but not an extreme one. The channel cross section may best be visualized by an example, for which Seneca Creek at Dawsonville, Maryland, will again serve.

Table 7 presents the data obtained from a leveling survey across the channel and valley flat near the gaging station on Seneca Creek. These data, representing elevations at different distances along the cross section, have been plotted in Figure 22. Note the tenfold exaggeration of the vertical scale.

The cross section shows that the valley flat at an elevation of approximately 225.5 feet mean sea level (msl) is nearly 200 feet wide on the left bank but is represented only by a narrow berm or flat place on the right bank.

The elevation of the stream bed is approximately 219 feet; thus the mean height of the channel bank is $225.5 - 219.0 =$

Table 7
Cross section across valley floor, Seneca
Creek at Dawsonville, Maryland

DISTANCE (FT)	ELEVATION (FT MSL)
0 + 00	228.0
0 + 25	225.3
0 + 50	225.5
0 + 75	225.3
1 + 00	225.1
1 + 25	225.1
1 + 50	225.5
1 + 75	226.2
1 + 85	226.0
1 + 90	224.0
1 + 95	220.0
2 + 00	218.8
2 + 05	218.8
2 + 15	219.1
2 + 25	219.6
2 + 45	220.2
2 + 55	221.7
2 + 65	225.6
2 + 75	225.5
2 + 85	229.0
2 + 95	235.0

6.5 feet. The channel is approximately 50 feet wide at the base and 70 feet wide at the top.

The height of zero feet on the staff gage (gage datum) is 220.0 feet msl. From the cross section the bankfull stage, 225.5 feet, corresponds to a gage height of 5.5 feet. If the rating curve at a gage height of 5.5 feet is entered in Figure 14, the corresponding discharge value when the water surface is at the top of the banks and about to overflow the channel is 1,350 cfs.

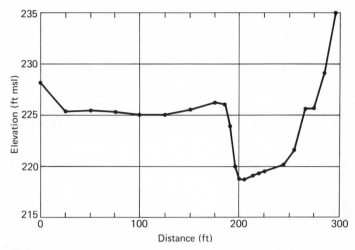

Figure 22
Cross section of channel and flood plain of Seneca Creek near the
gaging station at Dawsonville, Maryland. View is downstream.

There is another empirical way of estimating the discharge of
the bankfull condition. Studies of many rivers have revealed
that, with few exceptions, the bankfull discharge corresponds to
the recurrence interval of 1 to 2 years with an average of 1.5
years. This means that once every 1.5 years or 2 years out of 3,
on the average, the highest flow of the year will equal or exceed
bankfull.

If the flood frequency curve at a recurrence interval of 1.5
years is entered in Figure 21, the discharge value is 1,750 cfs.
This is in rough agreement with the bankfull discharge estimated
by inspecting the channel cross section and reading from the
rating curve (Fig. 14), which gave a value of 1,350 cfs.

A river flowing at bankfull will not be at the overflow level
everywhere along the channel because there are always slight
variations in height of bank or depth of channel resulting from
local conditions or chance causes. A typical view of a channel at
bankfull is shown in Figure 23, a reach of Watts Branch near
Rockville, Maryland. Note that the flat area in the foreground
is just being overflowed, but immediately upstream, in the middle
of the photograph, the flow is contained within the banks. This

Figure 23
Bankfull discharge in Watts Branch near Rockville, Maryland. The water is flowing just over the banks in the foreground, which is a point bar at the level of the flood plain. In the background, a terrace or former flood plain is standing approximately 1 foot above the water surface but is not overflowed by the discharge.

is because there is a terrace or abandoned flood plain bordering the channel at this point. This terrace stands approximately 1 foot above the flood plain and is not overflowed at the bankfull stage. The photograph was taken at the bankfull stage, that is, when the flood plain was just being covered with water.

6. The Flood Plain and the Channel

THE FLOOD PLAIN

Why is not the channel naturally made large enough to carry the largest flows without overflow? To answer this question it is necessary to determine how the channel is formed and what relation it bears to the adjoining valley floor or flat area, which is called the *flood plain*.

Most creeks or rivers flow in a definite channel bordered on one or both sides by a flat area or valley floor. With the exception of some mountain streams, nearly every river has areas that fit this description. These channels are seldom straight; bends or curves in a channel have an important effect on the manner of flow and the channel capacity.

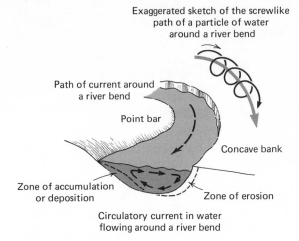

Figure 24
Effect of a curved channel on water flow. (U.S.G.S.)

As a flowing stream enters a bend in its channel (Fig. 24), the water at the surface, being swifter than that near the bottom, moves toward the concave bank and tends to erode it. Continuity requires, then, that surface water plunge downward near the concave bank and that some bed water emerge at the surface near the convex bank. This circulatory motion in the cross-sectional plane of a channel, which was first observed and explained by Thomson in 1879, is a result of the larger centrifugal force that is exerted on fast-moving surface parcels than on slower-moving ones near the bed. The motion gives to an individual water parcel a path resembling a helix.

The water near the bottom usually is carrying along some clay or sand or pebbles, and these are carried toward the inside of the curve by the slower-moving water. As indicated by the small arrows in the cross section (Fig. 24), water near the surface tends to move toward the concave bank and bed water tends to move toward the convex bank of the point bar. Thus material tends to accumulate on the convex edge of the bend and in so doing builds up the bed on that side, giving it a gradual slope.

The flow pattern of a meander is shown in Figure 25. The isometric view shows the two principal components of velocity at various positions in the bend. Because of the scale of the diagrams, the superelevation of the water surface in the bend is not shown but is implied by the velocity distribution.

The velocity in a meander crossover, or point of inflection, is not symmetrically distributed. As would be expected, proceeding downstream from the axis of the bend, the thread of maximum velocity is much closer to the concave bank than to the center of the channel. The high velocity, moreover, continues to hug this side through the point of inflection of the curve. At least in narrow channels, a cross-channel velocity component is directed toward the convex bank (usually called the point bar) near the bed and toward the concave bank near the surface.

The accretion of material on the point bar gradually pushes the convex bank into the channel and this tendency is compensated by the tendency of the concave bank to erode. Thus it is usual for a river channel gradually to migrate laterally across the valley floor. During such lateral migration the channel width remains the same.

If material is eroded off one bank of a channel and is deposited on the opposite bank, the channel moves gradually sideways. Because in most channels the bends are somewhat irregularly distributed along the length of the stream and the bends consist of curves both to the right and to the left, the progressive sideways movement of the channel is to the left in one place and to the right in another. Thus, given sufficient time, the channel eventually will occupy every position within the valley; each sideward motion leaves a flat or nearly level deposit that was caused by deposition on the inside of the curve. This flat bordering the channel is the flood plain, shown in the bottom diagram of Figure 26.

The present course of most rivers has not changed substantially in the past hundred years, but perhaps 500 years ago the channel was in quite a different place in the valley. Such movement is natural and results from the slow erosion on one side of a bend

84

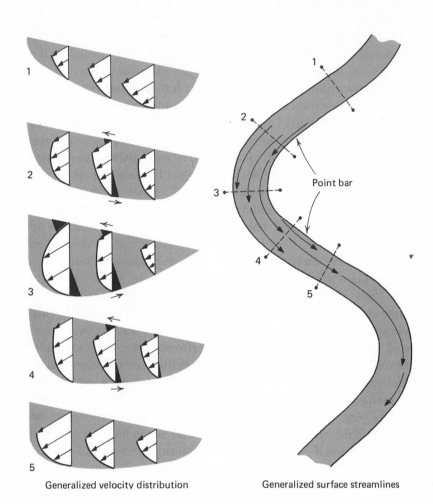

Generalized velocity distribution   Generalized surface streamlines

Figure 25
Isometric view of generalized diagram of flow distribution in a meander;
open parabolas with arrows indicate downstream velocity vectors; lateral
component of velocity is shown by gray areas; all sections are viewed from a
changing position to the left of and above the individual section. (From
Fluvial processes in geomorphology, by Leopold, Wolman, and Miller. W. H.
Freeman and Company. Copyright © 1964.)

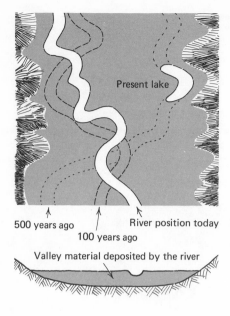

Figure 26
Present and past courses of a
reach, or length, of river.
(U.S.G.S.)

and the deposition on the opposite bank. Former positions of a
river are often indicated by the moon-shaped lakes that presently
exist on many flood plains (see Fig. 26).

Because deposition is taking place on one side as the river
moves laterally, the flood plain must have been formed to a great
extent by this deposition. In addition, considerable material is
deposited by floods on top of the flood plain. When the river is
in flood and water spreads over most of the whole valley floor,
sediment carried by the water is deposited in a thin layer over the
surface. These two processes account for the material making
up the flood plain.

The flood plain is formed by the material deposited on the
inside of channel bends and the material deposited when the
river overflows its banks, as indicated in the cross section through
the valley shown in the lower part of Figure 26. On top of the
bedrock or material undisturbed by the river, the valley is
covered with material deposited by the river. Such material
usually is a mixture of sand and silt, with some gravel.

Figure 27
The meandering gorge of the Colorado River at the Loop, below Moab, Utah. The channel has cut downward more than 1,000 feet since the Colorado Plateau area began to rise more than 1 million years ago. (U.S.G.S.)

There are instances where a meander bend persists for a long time, even many thousands of years, with virtually no point bar building and no appreciable lateral movement of the channel. The reason for this phenomenon is obscure, but an example of it is shown in Figure 27, which is a photograph of a meander loop of the Colorado River that maintained its shape with little lateral movement during the geologic period necessary to down-cut vertically 1,000 feet or more.

The building of a point bar balanced by bank erosion on the opposite side of the stream is demonstrated by a series of observations of Watts Branch, a small stream near Washington, D.C., for which cross sections were resurveyed over a 20-year period. Selected examples are presented in Figure 28.

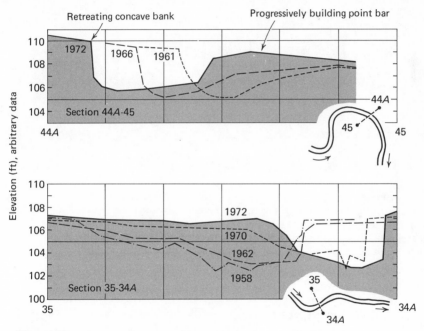

Figure 28
Data obtained from successive resurveys of Watts Branch near Rockville, Maryland, show lateral migration of a river channel by the building of a point bar into the stream and the concurrent erosion of the opposite bank. The continuation of such point bar building results in the development of a flood plain. Diagrams in lower right indicate position of the cross section relative to channel bends. (From Leopold, *Bull. Geol. Soc. America*, June 1973.)

Figure 29
Meander bend of Buffalo Creek, near Gardenville, New York. House in foreground stands on a terrace several feet higher than the flood plain. The flood plain level is the forested area within the bend in the center of the photograph. The sandy area without vegetation on the convex bank is newly deposited material of a building point bar. (Photograph by G. S. Smith, United States Soil Conservation Service.)

The upper diagram of Figure 28 shows successive positions of the channel during an 11-year period. It can be seen how the nearly flat surface of the point bar (right-hand side of the channel) is built by deposition, tending to force the channel to the left bank, which is the concave bank on a bend. The lower diagram shows an example of channel movement that is accompanied by the construction of a flat flood plain on the left bank.

Another example of point bar building along the convex bank is shown in the aerial photograph of Buffalo Creek, near Gardenville, New York, in Figure 29.

The manner in which a channel moves across the valley floor, eroding one bank and building a nearly flat flood plain on the other, while maintaining a cross section constant in shape and size, is an aspect of the dynamic equilibrium that characterizes many channel systems.

THE SIZE OF THE RIVER CHANNEL

Erosion on one bank and deposition on the other are approximately equal on the average, and gradual movement of the channel over the whole valley takes place without any appreciable change in the size of the channel.

The channel is constantly shifting position, though slowly, and the valley floor, or flood plain, is actually the result of this shifting. As long as the river is continually making its channel, why is the channel not made large enough to carry all the water without overflow?

In most regions of the world, daily rainfall is the exception rather than the rule. Light rains occur more frequently than do moderate ones; a heavy downpour occurs infrequently. A river channel will have only a moderate or small amount of water flowing in it on most days. On a few days each year there is usually sufficient rain or snowmelt to raise the river to a peak that just fills the channel but does not overtop its banks. The great amounts of flow that cause the largest floods usually occur very seldom. The river channel is shaped principally by the more frequent moderate flood flows, and it is large enough to accommodate these. Overflow of the flood plain takes care of the water of rare major floods that cannot be carried within the channel.

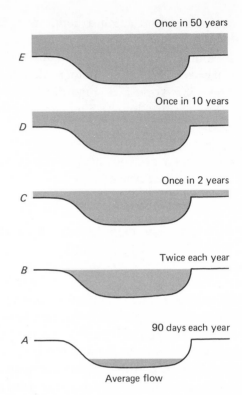

Figure 30
Amount of water in a river
channel and frequency with
which such an amount
occurs. (U.S.G.S.)

Figure 30 shows a cross section of a river and some of the flows
that can be expected at different intervals. Figure 30*A* shows the
river at average flow. During approximately 90 days of the year
there is no more water than is shown in *A*.

A heavy rainfall is required to produce enough surface runoff
to fill the channel to the top of the banks. Such rains occur
approximately twice each year. The level of the water, or bankfull
flow, that might be expected at these times a year is shown in
Figure 30*B*.

Less frequently, a storm will occur that will cause the river to
flow over the flood plain or valley flat. Approximately once every
2 years the river will overflow the flood plain to a depth shown
in Figure 30*C*. The depth over the flood plain in Figure 30*C* is

equal to the usual depth of water in the channel at average flow, shown in Figure 30*A*.

The heaviest, least frequent flows cover the flood plain even deeper. But the largest flood expected in a period of 50 years (Figure 30*E*) would be required to flood the whole flood plain to a depth equal to the height of the stream bank exposed by average flow.

The great, really catastrophic, flood may occur this year, next year, or the next. Such a flood might occur only once in several generations. Great floods occurred in New England in 1955 and again with hurricane Agnes, which hit the eastern United States in 1972. So extraordinary was the rainfall that fell during these disasters that it might not be repeated in another 1,000 years.

The chance of experiencing a great flood is similar to playing bridge. The game may be played often, but most players have never been dealt 13 cards of the same suit. Yet they know that they might get such a hand in the next game. So it is with floods. The very unusual event may occur tomorrow, but it is unlikely.

RIVER TERRACES

Erosional forces acting on an uplifted land mass tend to reduce it through time. Rivers as well as hillslopes tend to downcut gradually, while maintaining certain relationships along the river length. But the rate of downcutting is generally slow enough to allow processes causing lateral movement of the channel to operate, thus resulting in the formation of flood plains in the valleys of most rivers and creeks. These flood plains vary in width, depending on the size of the river, the relative rates of downcutting, and the hardness or resistance of the rock material in the valley walls. Flood plains may occur in the valleys of creeks or torrents even a few feet wide but are generally absent along the most headwater tributaries, presumably because downcutting is sufficiently rapid that time is not sufficient for lateral movement of any magnitude.

Figure 31
Flood plain of Blackrock Creek at Togwotee Pass, above Dubois, Wyoming.
The stream meanders broadly across the flood plain, which is confined
within steep valley sides bordered by a terrace.

Flood plains tend to be absent from most headwater channels
but often appear at the point where flow in the channel changes
from ephemeral to perennial—that is, where ground water
enters the channel in sufficient quantity to sustain flow throughout nonstorm periods. Perennial flow is influential in promoting
rock weathering along the stream margin and sloughing into the
channel, thus promoting lateral deposition and erosion along the
small stream.

During any period, then, when climatic characteristics remain
approximately constant, and in the absence of uplift or change of
base level, downcutting is slow enough that lateral swinging of
the channel can usually make the valley wider than the channel
itself. However, the elevation of the channel can be changed
episodically because of alteration of tectonic (especially mountain-building) and climatic factors.

In such a circumstance the flood plain level previously associated with the stream is abandoned, either by downcutting or by aggradation. During downcutting the previous flood plain is dissected, and portions may remain as continuous benches bordering the river or, more often, as remnants of flat or nearly flat spurs jutting into the river valley.

An example is shown in Figure 31, which is a photograph of the flood plain of Blackrock Creek, Wyoming. The river meanders on a flat flood plain or valley floor. This valley floor is hemmed in on both sides by a steep escarpment that represents the edge of a terrace or abandoned flood plain. The terrace forms the flat surface seen as the horizon in the photograph.

For present purposes a *terrace* will be defined as an abandoned flood plain. A terrace is composed of two parts, the scarp and the stair tread above and behind it. The term "terrace" is usually applied to both the scarp and the flat tread—that is, to the whole feature of the landscape. ("Terrace" is also not infrequently used to include or to mean the deposit itself, when alluvium rather than bedrock underlies the tread and riser. This deposit, however, should more properly be referred to as a fill, alluvial fill, or alluvial deposit, to differentiate it from the topographic form.)

The *flood plain* is the surface being constructed by the existing stream. It is not a terrace, although it is the surface of a formation composed of alluvial material. *Alluvial fill*, in the present context, is a deposit of unconsolidated or partially consolidated river-laid material in a stream valley, and it is a single stratigraphic unit.

The stages in the development of a terrace are diagrammed in Figure 32. Two possible sequences of events are shown that lead to the same surface configuration. Diagram *A* shows a river flowing on a flood plain. A change of climate or tectonic (mountain-building) warping could cause the river to degrade or cut into the material on which it has been flowing. At this lower elevation, given time, lateral swinging of the channel develops a new flood plain, leaving the former flood plain as a pair of terrace remnants bordering the valley.

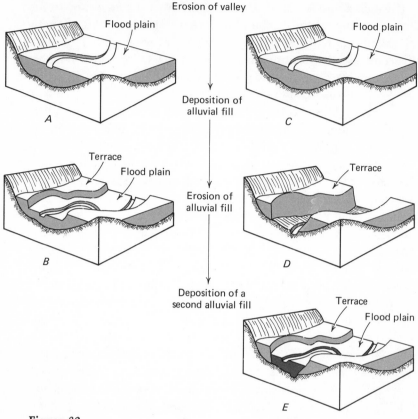

Figure 32
Block diagrams illustrating the stages in development of a terrace. Two sequences of events leading to the same surface geometry are shown in *A*, *B*, and *C*, *D*, *E*, respectively. (From *Fluvial processes in geomorphology*, by Leopold, Wolman, and Miller. W. H. Freeman and Company. Copyright © 1964.)

An alternative sequence is erosion (degradation or lowering), which is shown to occur between diagrams *C* and *D*. This is followed by aggradation (deposition or rise of river bed elevation) and the river flowing on alluvium of its own construction. The abandoned flood plain, now a terrace, consists of flat surfaces bordering the valley.

An example of two terraces is shown in Figure 33. The level or flat benches in the middle background and on the horizon are terraces.

The point to be stressed here is that a terrace is an abandoned surface not related to the present stream. The sequence of events leading to the observed features in the field may include several periods of alluvial deposition and thus several alluvial fills. If incision and aggradation occur repeatedly, it is possible to develop any number of terraces. Depending on the magnitude and sequence of the deposition and erosion, any number of fills of different stratigraphic units can be deposited.

Figure 33
Terraces along Rio San Cristobal near Lamy, New Mexico. The lower terrace is at a level approximately 5 feet above the present stream bed. A higher terrace makes up the horizon in the background.

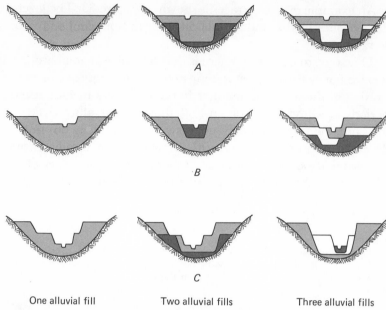

One alluvial fill   Two alluvial fills   Three alluvial fills

Figure 34
Examples of valley cross sections showing some possible stratigraphic
relations in valley alluvium: *A*, no terrace; *B*, one terrace; *C*, two terraces.
(From *Fluvial processes in geomorphology*, by Leopold, Wolman, and Miller.
W. H. Freeman and Company. Copyright © 1964.)

It should be noted that several alluvial fills can comprise the
valley sediments, even when no evidence of a terrace exists.
Three examples are given in Figure 34*A*. They demonstrate the
principle that any alluvial terrace is a former level of the flood
plain of a river.

Successive periods of erosion and deposition lead to the formation of river terraces and subsequent dissection. Such a sequence
thus provides a method of reconstructing a history of past events
that is especially useful in archaeology. The relation of the arti-
facts of man to their stratigraphic position in alluvial terrace
deposits has been of major importance in promoting knowledge
of ancient peoples.

Figure 35
Terrace comprised of two ages of material. The flat top, where growing plants can be seen, was once a flood plain. Later the stream lowered, cutting a wide, deep channel in the deposit and making the former flood plain into a terrace. The climate subsequently changed again and the channel was filled with the dark material seen in the center of the photograph. The river is the Rio Puerco, near Gallup, New Mexico. (From Leopold and Snyder, U.S.G.S. Water Supply Paper 1110-A, 1951.)

An example of a stratigraphic sequence that was closely re-lated to pottery shards and thus to the interpretation of the relation of climatic events to occupancy by early man is shown in Figure 35. Pottery remnants or shards whose dates could be determined from the design and the glaze were found to be associated with the alluvial fill that appears as a filled channel in the exposure provided by the arroyo wall pictured in Figure 35. The sequence of events causing erosion and deposition could be derived from the combination of dated pottery and the relation of alluvial fills and terraces.

Another example of the relation of flood plain to terrace is shown in Figure 36. In most field situations, as in this photograph, the vegetative association on the flood plain differs from that on the terrace. Here on Lance Creek, the flood plain is grassy and has groves of cottonwood trees, whereas the terrace, being farther from the stream and high above the local water table, supports a sagebrush cover. This is typical of many alluvial valleys of the western United States.

Figure 36
Terrace (*in background*) and flood plain of Lance Creek near Lance Creek, Wyoming. The flood plain is flat, grassy, and sparsely wooded with cottonwood trees.

Figure 37
Terrace and flood plain along an ephemeral stream in a semiarid area. The
terrace level at the right is approximately 4 feet above the present channel
bed. Rod held by the man indicates the flood plain level. The flood plain,
2 feet above the stream bed, has a different type of vegetation than the
terrace. The channel is Arroyo de Los Frijoles, near Santa Fe, New Mexico.

Still another relationship of terrace and flood plain, this one
typical of northern New Mexico and Arizona, is shown in Figure
37. The flood plain is obscure because its top surface is narrow
and irregular rather than flat, and is difficult to see because of
the brush growing on it. The terrace, 2 feet higher, is vegetated
with piñon-juniper trees and grass and is easily perceived as a
flat surface near the channel.

7. The Load of Rivers

THE SEDIMENT LOAD

When it rains or when snow thaws, the water in a river becomes muddy because it is carrying sediment that it has accumulated on its way over the land and through the stream channels. Water in nature is nearly everywhere in contact with the soil, but the amount of sediment carried is not the same in all streams and at all times.

When water is to be used for city supply or for many industries, sediment in the water is troublesome. It must be removed and then disposed of.

When a reservoir is constructed by damming a river, the sediment load of the river tends to deposit in the still water of the lake. Over time, sediment may fill a reservoir, using up the storage space intended for flood control, irrigation, power, or municipal supply. Whenever water is handled, sediment is also handled.

But though sediment in rivers often seems a costly nuisance when water is utilized, the river channel is accustomed to carrying sediment as well as water. When man changes the sediment load of streams by his works, the channel adjusts itself to accommodate the change just as a human body adjusts to seasonal changes in weather, to new bacteria, to new diet. When a person moves to a different altitude or climate, or changes his dietary environment, changes of metabolic rate, water loss, and other subtle adjustments occur. The river similarly adjusts to changes in sediment load or water discharge. Before the nature of these adjustments and their reasons are discussed, some of the native properties of sediment and the action of sediment in water will be considered.

Various kinds of sediment occur in streams. These vary in size of particle, shape (round, oblong, and angular), and kind. The most common mineral in river sediment is quartz, the same material that constitutes both common sand and table glassware.

An important characteristic of a sediment is the size of the grains. Most of the words used to describe different sediments are familiar and are used in everyday mention of earth materials. Coarse sediments are usually called gravel. Finer sediments are described as sand, silt, and clay. The smaller the particle, the greater is the surface of the grain relative to its weight. A 1-inch pebble has a surface area of approximately 3 square inches. If a 1-inch pebble is broken up into particles of clay size, each about 1/10,000 inch, the total surface area of the particles is 30,000 square inches. The surface area of a grain determines many of its physical properties, such as rate of settling, as well as its chemical activity.

If a quart bottle or large jar is filled with water and a handful of soil is added, the water immediately becomes muddy. If the bottle is shaken vigorously and set down, the soil particles begin

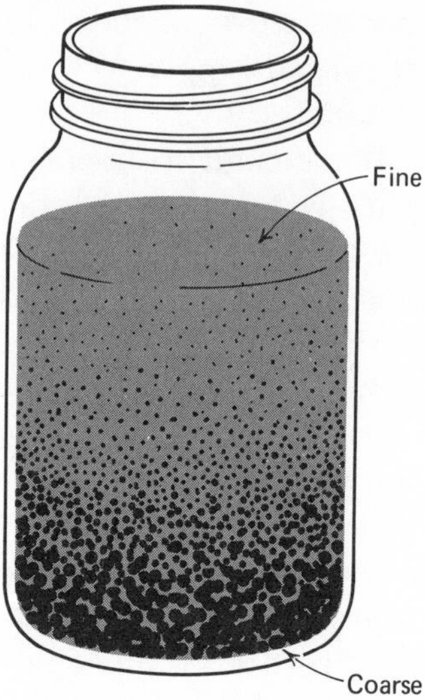

Figure 38
Sorting of fine and coarse sediment particles
settling in water. (U.S.G.S.)

to settle. The large particles settle to the bottom first; the very
fine particles settle slowly and may remain in suspension for a
long time. Several hours or days may be required for the water
to clear. The accumulation of soil at the bottom of the jar varies
from coarse particles at the bottom to fine at the top, as can be
seen in Figure 38. The rate at which particles settle in water is
determined by their size and weight.

In the jar the process of settling took place while the water was
still. However, in a moving stream the motion of flow keeps stir-
ring up the water and the particles of sediment may be carried
along by the water rather than settle out. The river water is
being shaken up continuously just as though the bottle were
shaken continuously. If the bottle were shaken gingerly and not
too rapidly, the fine particles would be kept in suspension and
the coarse ones would settle to the bottom.

Turbulent swirls in a mountain torrent can keep larger
particles in suspension than can less turbulent action in a big
river. Mountain torrents have adjusted their steep slopes to move

the large rocks that get into the channel from weathering of bed-rock. As travel down the river system breaks the rocks into smaller bits, into sand and finally silt, the channel is adjusted in width, depth, and slope to handle the sediment that is received from the river system upstream. The increases in river width and depth downstream are caused by the increasing amount of water as the river gets larger and also by the changes in amount and size of sediment. Not very much is known about how and why the river channel is the size that it is.

The sediment or rock debris carried by streams is derived from the weathering of rocks on the land. In the headwater areas of mountains, even large rocks can be moved downhill by the com-bined action of slow creep and moving water. The longitudinal profile of a river is steep in its headwaters, less steep in the middle course, and of gentle gradient still further downstream. This decreasing gradient is related in a general but complex way to the size of the material in the river bed, which also decreases downstream.

The mode by which large rock particles and small rock particles are carried by running water also differs, although again, size is not the only determinant.

Generally, the larger particles move as bed load and the small ones move as suspended load. *Bed load* is that portion of the mov-ing grain load whose immersed weight is carried by intermittent contact with the unmoving bed. The weight of bed grains can be compared to that of a tennis ball that is dribbled or succes-sively bounced off the floor. The floor must ultimately carry the weight of the ball even though the contact between the two is intermittent. Bed load includes the particles that roll, jump, skip, or saltate in an interrupted motion near the bed, never rising very far off the bed.

Suspended load is that part of the moving load whose weight is carried by the column of water in which it is immersed. This water does not stand directly on the surface of the unmoving grain bed but is supported by the water within the interstices of the bed grains. The turbulence in the flowing water of the channel keeps swirling the suspended grains upward in successive eddies. Between these intermittent upward lifts the suspended grains fall by gravity through the water at a rate dependent on their size.

The suspended load, then, is like a fleet of gliders or sail planes that slowly sink down through the air until an updraft gives them another upward increment. The sail planes are supported on the column of air by the updrafts just as suspended particles are kept up in a river by the similar turbulent eddies.

In most rivers the load in motion is carried less as bed load than as suspended load. The percentage of the total load in motion carried as bed load is generally in the range of 10 to 30 percent.

The load carried by rivers varies greatly from stream to stream. It is affected by the amount of rainfall. Differences in kinds of rock affect amount of sediment. Watersheds composed of fine windblown soil, as in western Iowa, put a large amount of sediment in the channel during every rainstorm and yield as much as 2,000 tons from each square mile in a year. Streams draining hard rocks, such as those in the Adirondack Mountains of New York State, carry very little sediment, usually less than 100 tons per square mile per year. Finally, plant cover on the land governs sediment yield. Barren areas produce vastly more sediment than tree-covered ones.

The rate of erosion of soil or rock debris from an area of land does not equal the load carried by a river downstream. The erosion rate is considerably greater than the downstream transport rate because there are many intermediate zones where sediment is deposited or stored. For very small plots or fields near a watershed divide, such as areas of .01 square mile (6 acres), perhaps 25 percent of the eroded material can be measured as sediment load in the river. For still larger basins the percentage drops even more. Eroded material is dropped on large areas of flood plains and at the bases of hillslopes, so rivers do not carry away to the ocean more than a small portion of what is annually eroded from the drainage basin surface. Through geologic time, however, a continent is ultimately eroded and dissolved, its surface becoming lower, as the transport processes carry the materials to the ocean through the action of flowing water.

When a dam is built across a river and sediment settles in the still water of the reservoir, clear water is released to the channel downstream. But the channel was accustomed to water containing some sediment. Therefore, the clear water causes the channel to change its shape and slope. These changes in channels downstream from dams cannot yet be accurately predicted because of lack of knowledge, but the changes are causing considerable difficulty to engineering works (dams, barriers, and bridge piers).

THE SALTS IN WATER

The chemical nature of water is important to man. Drinking water should not taste salty or of sulfur or iron, but neither should it taste flat like distilled water. It should also be soft enough to lather easily. It is the dissolved chemical compounds called salts that give water its taste and that make it either hard or soft.

The presence of calcium and magnesium compounds makes water hard because the calcium and magnesium combine with soap to form insoluble matter that deposits in the weave of the cloth being washed. This matter is extremely difficult to remove, and after continual washing in hard water, white sheets and clothes become the much advertised "tattle-tale gray."

There is great variety of kinds and amounts of salts in water, and their effects may be vastly different. Table salt, or sodium chloride, which is only one of the many kinds of salts, gives some water a salty taste. Some salts make water hard; yet these same salts can be helpful to irrigation. Others can ruin the soil if used for irrigation, and one type can poison crops. One salt that can mottle teeth can also protect them from decay if the amount is right.

Rainfall, though not chemically pure, is nearly pure water. As it falls it is at its purest moment in the entire hydrologic cycle. It contains dust material washed out of the air, salt carried inland from sea spray, and, most important, carbon dioxide. When rain strikes the ground it immediately comes in contact with many kinds of soluble materials. Rocks are composed of minerals, most of which are practically insoluble in water. During long periods, appreciable amounts are dissolved. The solvent action of water is increased by the carbon dioxide absorbed from the air. Many chemical elements are taken into solution by the water trickling and flowing through and over the rocks and the soil. Furthermore, new chemical compounds are formed when these elements meet in solution.

The chemistry is complex, but one source of dissolved matter in water can be illustrated by observing what can happen to one common mineral, feldspar. This is one of the minerals that make up the rock known as granite. One kind of feldspar contains oxygen, silicon, aluminum, and sodium. Among these elements sodium is held least tightly to its chemical partners, and so it is removed first in solution. Few elements are dissolved in pure or unattached form; rather, they join with some other element or combination of elements to form a new compound. Feldspar is therefore a source of sodium and silicon in water. Other minerals produce a wide variety of compounds when dissolved in water.

A typical compound, sodium bicarbonate, is formed by the attachment of sodium to some of the carbon dioxide that the rainwater picks up while passing through the atmosphere. Ground water commonly contains carbon dioxide and could therefore be called a weak carbonated water. The fizz in a carbonated drink is made up of dissolved carbon dioxide.

Some rocks are more soluble than others. Lava is relatively insoluble. Limestone and gypsum are very soluble; when they are exposed to the action of flowing water, they dissolve and thus are a source of calcium, carbonate, and sulfate. Solution of limestone forms caves. Carlsbad Caverns in New Mexico and Mammoth Cave in Kentucky are examples of the fantastic shape and size that may result from solution.

The quantity of mineral matter carried by water depends chiefly on the type of rocks and soils with which the water comes in contact, but the length of time of the contact is also important. Ground water usually contains more dissolved mineral matter than surface water because ground water remains in contact with rocks and soils for longer periods. Most streams are fed by both surface water and ground water. River waters therefore generally reflect the chemical character of ground water during dry periods. Because river waters carry less dissolved material during rainy periods or when there is heavy snowmelt, river water varies more in chemical character than ground water.

As previously mentioned, rainwater is almost pure. It usually contains less than 10 parts per million of dissolved matter; that is, 1 million pounds of water contains 10 pounds of dissolved material. This matter increases steadily as the water flows through the hydrologic cycle and reaches a maximum in evaporation basins such as the oceans, from which distilled water is returned to the air.

The dissolved material in rivers is usually less than 500 parts per million but some rivers may contain 2,000 or more parts per million. For the public water supply of a city, a concentration of more than 500 parts per million is considered undesirable. This would be comparable to approximately one quarter of a level teaspoon of salt in each gallon.

Some ground water, called brine, contains more than 10,000 parts per million of salt and is much too salty for most uses. Sea water contains 35,000 parts per million (3.5 percent) of salt. At a low stage, Great Salt Lake is nearly saturated and contains approximately 250,000 parts per million (25 percent) of common salt; this means that 1,000 pounds of lake water contains 250 pounds of salt in solution.

As water is heated to the boiling point, the dissolved salts do not leave with the vapor but are left in the pan. They tend to deposit on the walls of the container in which the water is heated. Heat tends to drive off some of the carbon dioxide gas that had helped dissolve the material from the rocks through which water passed. When the carbon dioxide is driven off, the material derived from the rocks is thrown out of solution and accumulates on the wall of the tea kettle. This also happens in hot water tanks in homes and in the boilers in industrial plants. The coating, or "scale," is similar to limestone. When deposited on the walls of a tank or boiler, it not only takes up space but adds markedly to fuel costs. A coating one-eighth inch thick makes it necessary to use 10 percent more fuel.

Sodium is an element that causes trouble on irrigated farms. Sodium salts tend to make a soil sticky when wet and to form clods when dry, with the result that plants absorb water only with difficulty. It also exerts harmful effects on plant growth. Calcium, which makes water hard and thus less desirable in home and factory, generally is beneficial in irrigation farming, for it tends to make the soil crumblike and thus easy for plant roots to grow and absorb water. Boron is one of several mineral constituents that are needed in very small amounts for plant growth. In large amounts, however, boron is poisonous to plants. Small amounts of fluorine in water tend to prevent cavities in children's teeth, but in excessive amounts fluorine mottles and discolors the tooth enamel.

Chemically pure water has a flat taste, and for this reason people prize the taste of water from springs and wells that has "flavor" because of a small but significant amount of salts in solution.

Salts in natural waters may be harmful or beneficial, so it is important to know the amount and kind of salts in the water supply and how they affect the use of the water.

8. Soil, Plants, and Water

WATER IN RELATION TO SOIL

The part played by the soil in accepting or rejecting precipitation has already been described. Water rejected by the soil runs off into a stream; water that filters through the soil becomes soil moisture. If there is enough infiltration, some water reaches the water table. The soil thus occupies a key place in hydrology.

Plants grow best in dark, fine soil that crumbles easily between the fingers. Soil that is full of hard clods of light color will harden when it dries and the tender plants will not do well. The difference between good soil and poor soil is analogous to the difference between soil and rock. Soil differs from weathered rock in three principal ways: the presence of humus, the development of layers, and the formation of crumbs.

A good soil has plenty of humus, organic material containing small particles of decomposed plant material (originally small roots, leaves, and stems) that are broken down into bits that mix with the particles of mineral material, sand, and clay.

The action of air, rain, and solutes on rocks—that is, weathering—causes decomposition into small pieces. But weathered rock without humus will not produce large, healthy plants.

The process of weathering at the earth's surface has another effect. Water passing through the surface dissolves some parts of the rock material, slowly but surely. The dissolved material, like sugar in tea, is carried by the water. Thus the surface layer of soil material loses some ingredients, and deeper layers may gain those same ingredients. This process of movement by partial solution develops layers near the surface. Such layers can be seen in road cuts along the highway. A commonly found dark band right at the surface indicates that the uppermost layer has acquired some dark organic material, humus. The presence of humus implies that this layer has lost some mineral material by solution.

The changes accompanying this slow process of rock breakdown and development of layers also make the small individual particles of clay and silt stick together in crumbs. Between the crumbs are open spaces through which water may filter down. The accumulation of small particles into crumbs forms the *structure* of a soil. Humus is necessary for the development of a granular or crumb structure, which is desirable for growing plants because it allows space between the particles. These minute openings provide space not only for water and for the microscopic roots of plants, but also for air, which is as necessary for the growth of roots as it is for the growth of leaves, stems, and flowers. Many house plants grown in glazed or metal flower pots die because water fills all the spaces between the soil particles and the roots cannot get air. Roots that are completely submerged may literally drown.

To give weathered rock the properties of soil requires many years or even several lifetimes. Each of these requisites (humus, layering or profile development, and structure) depends on more than the presence of vegetation. Millions of different kinds of insects that live in the soil all play their part. The worms and grubs that are visible are very few in number compared with minute bacteria, fungi, and microscopic forms of life. Most of these minute organisms live on the dead remains of plants and actually carry out the decay of the old leaves, stems, roots, and other plant parts. The soil, therefore, is not merely broken-up rock. It is a whole world of living things, most too small to be seen. It is a constantly changing layer, losing some of its constituents and gaining others. This constant exchange in the soil keeps it in the form most useful to man—good for growing plants and capable of absorbing and holding water.

VEGETATION AND WATER

Plants take up from the soil not only water but dissolved mineral material that is necessary for the building of the plant cells. The dissolved materials that are used by the plants are called mineral nutrients. They are, in a way, the food for the plants.

With sunlight and water the green leaves of the plant make sugars, which, in turn, are changed to the starches and other plant material in the form of potatoes, beans, rice, and other foods. These nutrients are provided by the soil.

How much of a plant, such as a tree, is made up of the mineral nutrients from the soil? When a log is burned in the fireplace, the amount of remaining ash is very small compared with the original log. The ash contains nearly all the mineral nutrients. By far the greater part of the log that went up the chimney as smoke consisted of water and of the organic material manufactured in the leaves. Thus the soil provides only a small part of the plant, but a most essential part. It also provides the medium in which the plant can extend its roots and absorb water.

Soil water is absorbed and transpired by plants. This use of water by plants results in soil becoming drier to much greater depths than if the soil were bare and water merely evaporated from the surface. Roots extract most of the available water from the soil in which they are growing. In some areas, plant roots grow to depths of several feet. In arid parts of the western United States, some roots grow as deep as 50 feet. Evaporation from a bare soil surface will dry the soil to depths of only 1 or 2 feet.

Anyone who has tried to grow shrubbery around the house or a few tomato plants and lettuce in the backyard knows that in the spring the soil is so wet that digging in it is a most unpleasant chore. In late summer, however, this soil is so dry and hard that digging in it is almost impossible. Again, in autumn after plants shed their leaves and become dormant, the soil becomes wet. This conspicuous seasonal change in soil moisture is partly the result of the use of water by plants. They use large quantities in summer and almost none in winter.

Besides the seasonal cycle, there is a daily cycle in the use of water; that is, between day and night of a summer day. Plants transpire, or lose, most water during a hot, dry, sunny day but lose very little at night. This daily variation in water loss is reflected in the flow of water in small streams draining areas of a few hundred acres in size. If no rain has fallen for several days, streamflow is highest in the morning hours, reflecting the low rate of water use during the preceding nighttime.

SOIL EROSION

All the water that comes from the atmosphere as precipitation must pass through or over the top layers of the earth, and nearly everywhere this top layer is the soil. Soil erosion and the need to conserve soil are crucial contemporary problems. Erosion is caused principally by water, and therefore no general discussion of water would be complete without consideration of its relation to the soil-erosion problem.

Some soils take in water more easily than others. The more precipitation is infiltrated into the soil, the less will run off the surface, and thus the tendency for soil loss by erosion is decreased. Vegetation tends to break the force of the falling raindrops and holds the soil particles together, thus tending to prevent the soil from washing away.

The incorporation of the plant material in the uppermost layer of the soil affects its ability to absorb water. A lush cover of vegetation does not necessarily indicate the presence of large amounts of humus in the soil. The jungles in some tropical countries, for instance, grow on soil that contains very little organic material because of the high rate of decomposition. Once the tropical forest is cut down, rains wash away the soil very quickly because there is nothing to keep the mineral particles from sticking together and closing the pores. Rain can beat down on a bare soil that contains much humus and still be rapidly absorbed.

The top layer of the soil erodes away first, and this top layer contains more of the nutrients that are necessary for plants and animals than do the deeper layers. Loss of the most fertile top soil is usually serious because in most areas it cannot be replaced except over long periods.

In some areas, the weathered material is deep and bedrock does not lie close to the surface but is found at great depth. Under such conditions, even after erosion has removed several feet of the top layers, sufficient material still remains in which plants can be grown. The loss of the top layers of a deep soil is less serious than loss from shallow soil.

Soils protected by growing vegetation tend to maintain their fertility and are resistant to the erosive force of rain and running water. The better soils generally produce the most nutritious crops. Thus a cover of vegetation tends to maintain high soil productivity and to minimize soil erosion bosses.

Soil probably could be best maintained by leaving the vegetation as it was originally; that is, with no interference by man. Yet man must grow crops to live and thus must expect a greater rate of soil loss than occurred under original conditions.

EFFECT OF LAND USE ON WATER

Because soils that are protected from erosion by plant cover are also those that absorb water best, soil conservation has frequently been confused with the control of great floods. One view is that floods can be prevented if soils are maintained in their best condition for the rapid infiltration of water. Surface runoff is the principal source of flood water; therefore, water that is absorbed in the soil will not run off. This argument may apply to small or moderate rains but does not apply to great floods, as will be discussed.

From a particular rain, a larger percentage of the total water will sink into a good lawn than will be infiltrated into the garden patch where the soil is bare. The bare soil in Figure 39A is absorbing water less rapidly than the ground surface of Figure 39B; thus there is more runoff from the bare area. The lawn would, in general, have a greater rate of infiltration and would be comparable to a sieve of large mesh. Corresponding to the fine mesh sieve, the bare garden patch would absorb some of the rainfall, but much would flow off and appear in the gutter as surface storm runoff. If the lawn could absorb the rainwater as fast as it fell, then none would run off.

In the same rainstorm, all the rain that fell on a roof or an impervious concrete driveway would run off into the gutter, so the gutter would get water as fast as it fell. Rates of runoff are greater in a given storm from areas having low infiltration rates. As discussed previously, rate of runoff is expressed as the number of gallons or cubic feet of water discharged per second or per minute.

The first water that infiltrates moistens the soil particles. If there is enough water to moisten the soil all the way down to the water table, any additional water infiltrating can pass downward and add to the amount of water in the saturated zone. The water that moistened the soil particles is retained in the soil and is gradually returned to the atmosphere by evaporation or transpiration during periods of fair weather.

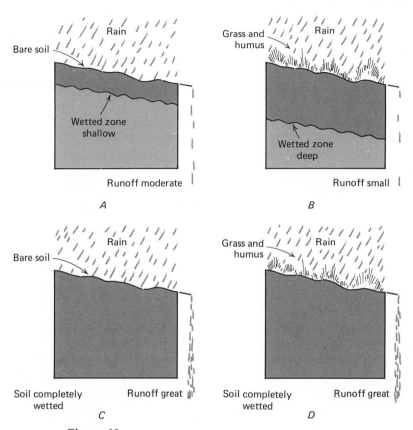

Figure 39
Runoff from bare and vegetated surfaces under different
conditions of soil moisture.

An increase in the infiltration rate caused by changes in the vegetation may, under some circumstances, result in an increase in the amount of water returned to the atmosphere by transpiration and thus reduce the proportion appearing in surface streams. In areas where there is considerable rainfall, such as the eastern United States, such changes would be relatively unimportant because there is a large amount of water available for surface flow.

In arid regions, however, increasing the amount of water lost to the atmosphere may appreciably change the small amount of runoff in surface streams.

Rainfall enters the soil by infiltration. When there has been enough rain to saturate the soil, further rainfall will be rejected and will run off into the streams. Therefore, improvements in vegetation or farming methods intended to increase the infiltration capacity of the surface will be most helpful over deep soils that have great capacity for receiving and retaining water. Continued rainfall does two things: It decreases the infiltration rate at the surface and it decreases the capacity of the soil body to absorb more water. This is shown in Figure 39C and D, in which both soils are completely wetted. Under this condition the amount of runoff from the grassed areas is approximately the same as from the bare one.

The most devastating floods occur at times when there is sufficient rainfall to saturate the soil. Such saturation may result from a long period of continuous moderate rainfall, such as a rainy period of several weeks, or it may occur at a time when snows have provided enough moisture to wet the soil thoroughly. When the soil is sufficiently wet, the infiltration rate for bare areas is only slightly different from that of well-vegetated areas; the capacity to receive and retain additional rainfall is essentially the same. Therefore, the amount of vegetation has little effect on the catastrophic flood because such a flood occurs only after a thorough wetting of the soil. Thus the great floods, such as those of the Ohio River in January 1937 and of the Kansas River in July 1951, are not affected by watershed management or soil conservation measures to any extent. When there is enough rain at high-enough intensities to produce a catastrophic flood, the rate of infiltration in an area that is farmed does not differ substantially from that of an uninhabited, wooded area. Many of the highest floods known occurred before man began logging or farming in the basins that produced the floods.

PART II

*Water Supplies
and Water Use*

9. The Water in the World

An intensive effort has been made by R. L. Nace to make a coherent estimate of the total amount of water in the world and its distribution. Interestingly, he has been able to show that if the flow of all the largest rivers in the world is totaled, the addition of successively smaller rivers makes less and less difference. The majority of the water involved in the hydrologic cycle of the earth is accounted for by emphasis on the large quantities, and the smaller additions and subtractions add mere detail to the whole picture.

The world's oceans contain more than 97 percent of all the water on earth, the staggering large total of 317 million cubic miles. Compared with this figure, all other locations are small. This fact is emphasized by Table 8, which shows that the fresh-water portion is only a small percentage. The seas are salt and

Table 8
Water on the earth

LOCATION	WATER VOLUME (CUBIC MILES)	PERCENTAGE OF TOTAL WATER
SURFACE WATER		
Fresh-water lakes	30,000	.009
Saline lakes and inland seas	25,000	.008
Average in stream channels	300	.0001
SUBSURFACE WATER		
Water in unsaturated aerated zone (includes soil moisture)	16,000	.005
Ground water within depth of 1/2 mile	1,000,000	.31
Ground water, deep lying	1,000,000	.31
OTHER WATER LOCATIONS		
Icecaps and glaciers	7,000,000	2.15
Atmosphere (at sea level)	3,100	.001
World ocean	317,000,000	97.2
Totals (rounded)	326,000,000	100

therefore of limited use for water supply. An appreciable part of the world's total, 2 percent, is frozen in the icecaps and glaciers. The antarctic icecap covers 6 million square miles and contains 85 percent of the frozen water. If this icecap were melted at a uniform rate, the 6 million cubic miles would feed the Mississippi for 50,000 years, or it would feed all the rivers in the United States for 17,000 years.

The water vapor in the atmosphere is derived from evaporation from oceans and land and from transpiration from plants. Approximately 95,000 cubic miles of water goes into the air annually as water vapor derived from these sources. Of this amount, 80,000 cubic miles represents the evaporation from the surface of the world's oceans.

Of the water that changes from liquid at the earth's surface to vapor in the atmosphere, 71,000 cubic miles falls back on the ocean and 9,000 cubic miles falls on land, furnishing the source of the flow of rivers and springs. The remaining 15,000 cubic miles infiltrates into the land surface and is available for absorption by plants and replenishment of ground storage.

10. The Water Budget

When a hydrologist or student of water studies the water supplies of an area, one of the first things he does is to set up a water budget—a balance sheet—of the receipts, disbursements, and water on hand. Existing information about water is rather spotty, and this makes it difficult to prepare a detailed day-to-day water budget for a watershed serving most towns or cities with water. However, there is enough information to estimate an annual budget for the United States as a whole.

The occurrence of water in the atmosphere and on and in the ground and oceans is summarized by Figure 40, which shows the water cycle and the items to be listed in the budget. Arrows directed toward the land surface designate the input or credit items in the budget. Those leading from the land indicate output

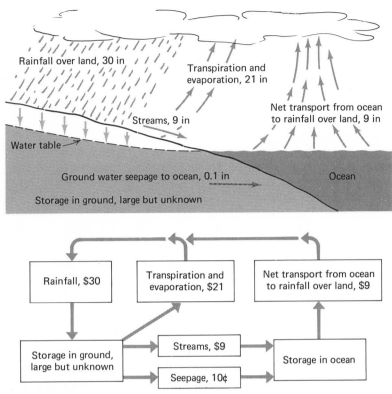

Figure 40
Water budget of the continental United States. (U.S.G.S.)

or debit items. The quantities could be expressed in various ways, such as gallons or cubic feet, but they are easier to understand if they are expressed in terms of inches of depth over the United States. Accordingly, 1 inch of water would be equivalent to the amount required to cover the country 1 inch deep. One inch over the United States would be equivalent to 161 million acre-feet or $5\frac{1}{2}$ times the storage capacity of Lake Mead, behind Hoover Dam.

In Figure 40, the inputs of water may be considered credit items; amounts of water withdrawn or depleted represent debit items:

Credit: The input is entirely in the form of rainfall and snowfall. This precipitation averages approximately 30 inches over the United States each year.

Debit: The removal of water from the land includes the flow of streams, deep seepage of ground water to the oceans, transpiration from plants, and evaporation from lakes, ponds, swamps, rivers, and from the moist soil.

The annual discharge of rivers to the sea amounts to 9 inches. It is interesting to note that of this 9 inches, 40 percent is carried by the Mississippi River alone. The amount of deep seepage from ground water to the sea is not known, but it is believed to be quite small, probably much less than 0.1 inch per year.

Evaporation from wet surfaces and transpiration from plants are similar processes and hydrologists often combine them and call the total *evapotranspiration.* The total evapotranspiration over the United States averages approximately 21 inches per year.

An examination of these figures reveals that for the land area of the continent, the water cycle balances as follows: credit, 30 inches; debit, 9 inches plus 21 inches. However, if the atmosphere is examined, the cycle appears out of balance because the atmosphere delivers 30 inches to the land as rain and snow but receives back only 21 inches as vapor from evapotranspiration. The atmosphere makes up this difference of 9 inches by transporting moisture from the oceans to the continent to balance the discharge of rivers to the sea.

Each year the atmosphere brings 150 inches of moisture from the oceans to the land, and each year it carries back 141 inches. Of the 30 inches that fell from the atmosphere to the land as precipitation, 21 inches returned as vapor to the atmosphere (by evapotranspiration) and 9 inches was carried to the oceans by rivers, later to be returned to the atmosphere. Thus precipitation and evaporation are only a part of the whole atmospheric movement of moisture across the continent.

The atmospheric moisture budget balances each year, but not much is known about the capital stock, that is, the amount in the lakes, in ground water, and in soil moisture. But the stock of water on hand is relatively stable. Most measurements have attempted to determine how the water stocks in different places change from season to season or from year to year rather than estimating the total amount. For example, from measurements it has been estimated that there is an average seasonal change in soil moisture of 4 inches per year in the eastern part of the United States. The seasonal range in ground-water storage in the eastern part of the country is approximately the same. Changes in soil moisture plus ground water add up to approximately 8 inches during the course of a year.

Seasonal fluctuation of water on hand is not very large (8 inches when changes in both soil moisture and ground water are considered). This seasonal variation is quite distinct from the total amount of water in the ground and in the soil. The total amount is very large, but available data are so meager that a meaningful estimate is quite impossible.

THE FLUCTUATING WATER SUPPLY

Because fresh water is derived from rainfall, water supplies are linked to the weather. Weather and streamflow are variable. In what respect is this variability important?

The thousands of cities that obtain their water supply from streams, the thousands of irrigators and hundreds of power-plant operators, all wish to know as much as possible about present and future fluctuations in flow. Measurements of river flows constitute streamflow records, which can be used to predict streamflow for short periods in advance. The principal considerations used in preparing a forecast are as follows.

Streamflow is derived from rainfall or snowmelt; the greater the amount of precipitation, the greater the streamflow. But infiltration into the soil has first call on available rainwater or snowmelt; the drier the soil, the greater is the amount of water retained by it. These two factors, the amount of precipitation and the state of soil moisture, determine the amount of runoff. To make a forecast, therefore, the hydrologist measures the precipitation and deducts from it the amount of water that will be retained by the soil. The difference between precipitation and retention is an estimate of the runoff.

However, the forecast can be made only after the precipitation has fallen on the ground. For the same reason, the forecast of streamflow applies only to the precipitation that is measured. Streamflow resulting from a rainstorm may be forecast only over the few hours or days that are required for a river to rise and subside. This is called flood forecasting. Forecasts of streamflow from the melting of a winter's accumulation of snow in the high mountains of the western United States may be made 2 to 4 months in advance. The snow reaches its maximum accumulation at the end of March. The melting does not occur until late spring or early summer. Thus snow surveys made in the early spring can give forecasts of the runoff over the warm months ahead.

Forecasts are useful, not only for operating irrigation works but for saving lives during floods. Yet these forecasts are only short-term. Long-range forecasts would allow water projects to be designed with maximum success.

Long-term changes

Fortunately, over the long run a given location will experience a pattern of wet and dry, hot and cold weather. But the pattern is not necessarily repetitive. Some of the changes are so well known that they have been named. Much of North America, as far south as New York City, was once covered by glacial ice.

This period is the well-known ice age. The weather was obviously colder and wetter than it is today. Desert areas in California, Nevada, and Utah were not deserts then, and many small and large lakes existed in places where now the weather is dry enough for horned toads and sagebrush.

The last advance of glaciers ended approximately 10,000 years ago. Since the ice melted, the climate has changed several times. Approximately 4,000 years ago the continent was warmer and drier than it is today. This period is called the Altithermal. Temperatures were so high that most of the mountain glaciers in North America and Europe disappeared completely.

Even in recent times there was a period of cold and wet. The mountain glaciers of western North America probably reached their maximum size in the late nineteenth or early twentieth century. At that time modern glaciers were larger than at present, and so the period is called the Little Ice Age. But for the past few decades the glaciers have been shrinking by melting. The weather during the first half of the twentieth century has shown a warming trend, in comparison with the period 1870–1900. In the 1950's, the warming trend began to slow, and some mountain glaciers again began to reach a little farther down their valleys.

Climatic changes through geologic time must have been very sharply marked and have lasted many centuries. The earliest records must be read in the rocks. Fossil plants and animals are a clue to the climate of that time. The deposits of sand and gravel in moraines, scour marks in hard rocks, and U-shaped valleys are records left by glaciers. The bones of arctic animals far south of their present habitat are also evidence of glacial cold.

When man appeared on the earth, he made tools and clothing that tell a story about the kind of weather that existed. After he learned to write, approximately 50 centuries ago, he wrote about his crops and left records that tell a more precise story. The development of science and scientific instruments have made possible the recording of rainfall and temperature and thus the direct measurement of climate. Some weather records go back 200 years. The longest record in the United States, that of the temperatures in New Haven, Connecticut, was begun about 1750, and was at first kept by physicians and clergymen who made the observations as a matter of personal interest and curiosity. The rainfall record at Santa Fe, New Mexico, was begun in 1849. It was kept originally by the physician at the Army post.

Most of geologic time was considerably warmer than the present climate of the earth. In relation to the ice age, the present climate is warmer; but it is cooler now than it was around A.D. 1000 when the Vikings settled in Greenland and reconnoitered along the northern coast of North America.

Variations in streamflow

Streamflow is what is left over after precipitation has supplied the demands of vegetation and the process of evaporation. Leftovers or differences tend to vary greatly with time. For example, suppose that the rainfall in one year is 40 inches and that evaporation and plant transpiration 20 inches. This leaves 20 inches to be carried off by the streams. Suppose that in the next year rainfall is 30 inches, 25 percent less than in the year before. If evaporation and transpiration were the same, which is quite possible, streamflow would be only 10 inches, 50 percent less than in the year before. Thus a 25 percent change in rainfall becomes a 50 percent change in runoff. This means that the flow of streams is highly variable and sensitive to changes in rainfall.

Figure 41 shows the variations in the flow of eight streams in different parts of the United States. Because year-to-year variations tend to mask any dominant pattern, the graphs show a 5-year moving average. Perhaps the major characteristic of these graphs is the high flows in the earlier parts of the records. Most of the graphs show a discernible downward trend that is most marked in the western streams.

During the period of record, the period of lowest streamflow in the United States occurred during the decade 1930–1940, with a fortunate upswing during the war years when there were rapidly mounting demands for water. In the late 1960's a downward trend again appeared.

Ever since record collection began, hydrologists have plotted graphs and wondered whether the ups and downs represent cyclic changes (changes that repeat again and again). For example, the graph for the French Broad River in North Carolina appears to be repetitive or cyclic. There are many cyclic changes in Nature, and nearly all are related to the day or year, day and night, and the four seasons of the year. The tides too are cyclic, and indeed daily tides are forecast years in advance.

Despite the success in forecasting tides, very little success has come from efforts to extend the apparent cycles in the long records of streamflow. At present it is known merely that these ups and downs are part of the pattern of streamflow and that variations as great or even greater can be expected. The downward trend, except as affected by uses of water and land, is not likely to persist indefinitely, but just when and in what manner changes will occur cannot be foretold. Tomorrow's weather can be forecast reasonably well; less accurate but useful forecasts of weather can be made 5 days ahead, and speculations can be made of the weather 30 days ahead. Long-term forecasts of weather or of streamflow are not yet possible.

The long-term future is judged by comparison with the past. Streamflow for the coming year cannot be accurately forecast, but past records can be used to predict the probability, for example, of a flood of any given height. Suppose that in the past 100 years, a given river reached a height of 50 feet 5 times, or an average of once in every 20 years. It is probable that in the next 100 years, that river will also reach the 50-foot stage 5 times, but when these 5 floods will come cannot be predicted. They could all come within one 20-year period.

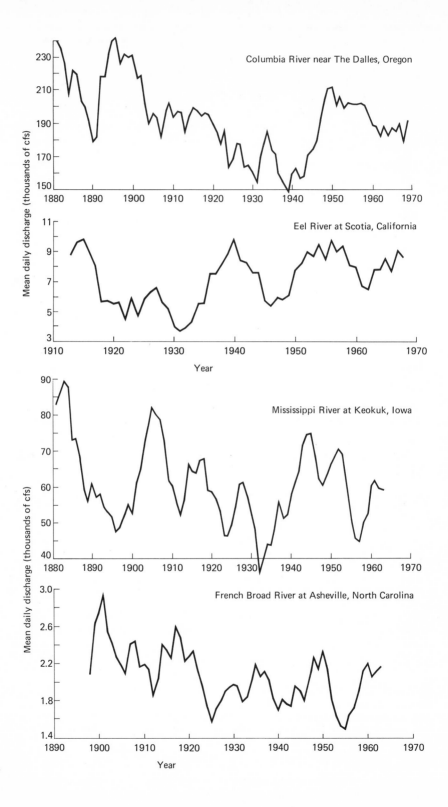

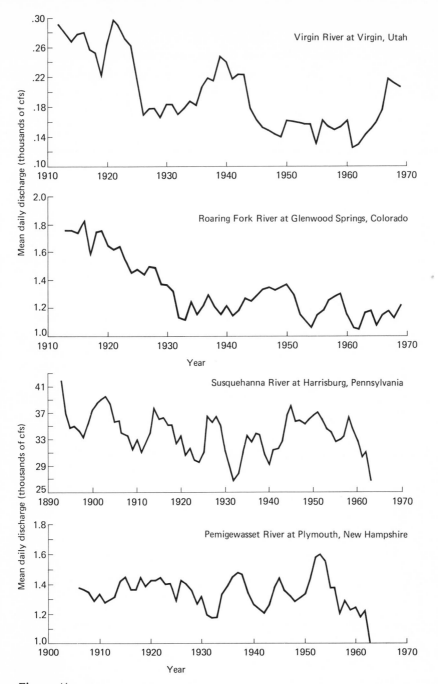

Figure 41
Graphs of streamflow over time for selected rivers in the United States. The data are 5-year moving averages. Note the nonrepetitive but variable character of the flow and the large differences among rivers, even during the same period.

An actual view of variability can be obtained by analyzing the yearly flows in the Columbia River. In the 90-year record of the river shown in Figure 41 (a rather long period as records go), yearly average flows have varied greatly. The greatest annual flow was 2.2 times the lowest annual flow. The averages of 10-year periods have also varied, but less, the greatest being 1.45 times the least. For 20-year periods the highest average was 1.3 times the lowest. Thus variability decreases as the length of the period increases, but variability never becomes zero. It is known that considerable variability remains between periods even as long as 200 years. When using streamflow records, allowance must be made for this variability (that is, the probability that the flow will be even more or even less than any previously experienced flow).

The water user is in a dilemma. If he limits his use to only a small part of the available water to be sure of his supply, then water goes by unused. If he tries to use too much of the available water, the risk of shortage becomes great. This is the general problem facing the United States as a consequence of the variable nature of streamflow. Because of variability of flow, all the water can never be put to use.

11. Amount of Water Available and Its Present Use

The United States as a whole receives an average of approximately 30 inches of precipitation annually; that is, the annual fall would cover the total land area to a uniform depth of $2\frac{1}{2}$ feet. Almost 3/4 of the total precipitated water is returned to the atmosphere by evaporation and transpiration. The remaining 1/4 contributes to runoff and ground storage and constitutes the water available for withdrawal use. This quarter that is available can be expressed as an average yield of 1,300,000 million gallons per day, which is equivalent to 7,500 gallons each day for every man, woman, and child in the United States, or approximately the amount that could be stored in a box 10 feet on a side.

Water that goes into ground storage or surface runoff is the total supply available to fill human demands. The rest is lost to the atmosphere. This total supply of 7,500 gallons per person each day is a relatively large amount. The United States is well blessed compared with most other countries.

In any discussion of the uses of water, it must be remembered that some uses result in actual consumption or loss of water to the atmosphere as vapor. For example, a gardener tries to sprinkle water near the plant roots. Because water taken up by the plant is transpired to the atmosphere as vapor, the water is consumed or lost to further use by man. Irrigation may, therefore, be called a *consumptive use* because to a great extent water is lost to further use.

In contrast, water used for such normal household purposes as bathing, dishwashing, and toilet flushing is not consumed but is mostly returned to the surface streams through the sewerage system. These are called nonconsumptive uses.

USE OF WATER

In the home

Water is used in the home mainly for drinking, cooking, washing clothes and dishes, and bathing. Other principal uses are for toilet flushing and lawn and garden sprinkling. Together these are called *domestic uses*. The average use per person in an American home varies between 20 and 80 gallons per day. Listed below are some typical figures on the amount of water necessary for certain home operations.

Flush a toilet	3 gallons
Take a tub bath	30 to 40 gallons
Take a shower bath	20 to 30 gallons
Wash dishes	10 gallons
Operate a washing machine	20 to 30 gallons

Water use in the author's home will furnish some specific examples. The Leopold family of four in suburban Washington,

D.C., used on the average 70 gallons per person per day, which included lawn sprinkling in summer. In that area, the charge for water is 27 cents per thousand gallons. For 70 gallons per person per day, then, the Leopold family paid $7\frac{1}{2}$ cents per day.

In Berkeley, California, the author's family used 80 gallons per day per person in the rainy season of winter. The amount increased to 200 gallons per person per day in summer when the garden was sprinkled. The charge for water in Berkeley is $46\frac{1}{2}$ cents per thousand gallons.

A charge of 27 cents per thousand gallons means a charge of $6\frac{1}{2}$ cents per ton of water delivered at the tap. Thus water is, as the saying goes, cheap as dirt. In fact, water is much cheaper than dirt. Delivery of a ton of dirt would cost several dollars rather than $6\frac{1}{2}$ cents.

Waste of water in the home can increase the bill by several dollars. A dripping faucet that leaks only one drop each second will waste 4 gallons a day. A leak into a toilet bowl, which is not seen but detected only as an unimportant hum in the pipe, may easily amount to $1\frac{1}{2}$ gallons per hour. This would be a waste of 13,000 gallons per year.

Most persons in eastern United States probably do not water their lawns as much as would be best for the grass. The irrigation need in the vicinity of Washington, D.C., is probably approximately 6 inches per year. An average yard of 8,000 square feet would thus require 30,000 gallons, which, at 27 cents per thousand, would cost approximately $8 per year.

In the cities

In many cities each home has a water meter to measure water use, and the consumer pays for just what he takes. Elsewhere a person pays a flat rate regardless of how much he uses. Water engineers have found that families are much more economical in the use of water when their use is individually measured by a meter. Families paying a flat rate use, on the average, twice as much water as those whose use is metered.

Water use varies during the day and during the week in a way that reflects some interesting details of American home life. Use is, of course, low during the night but increases rapidly to a maximum between 8 and 9 o'clock in the morning. Another peak use occurs between 6 and 8 o'clock in the evening. Though there is variation in maximum peak between cities, this difference is interpreted to mean that more people take baths in the morning than at bedtime. Also, an extra heavy peak occurs on Saturday night in many cities; so it appears that the Saturday night bath is still a reality.

Though water use in the home is usually thought of as the principal reason for the existence of a municipal system, industries are the major users of water from municipal systems. Many industrial plants find it more economical to buy water from the city than to provide individual supplies from wells or reservoirs. The average water use for industrial purposes from public supplies can best be stated in relation to the population of the city. Average use by commerce and industry is approximately 70 gallons per capita per day.

In addition to domestic and industrial uses, there are two other main classes of water use of municipal supplies: public use, which includes fire extinguishing, street cleaning, public-building use, and maintenance of public parks, and which accounts for approximately 10 gallons per capita per day; and loss or unaccounted-for waste. Leaks from the water mains and unmeasured leaks from faucets, as well as errors of measurement, contribute to this loss. This item is amazingly large, and generally even careful construction and management cannot reduce it to less than 20 percent of the total use.

In total, the average use of water per capita in American cities was approximately 150 gallons per day in 1960, having risen progressively with the increase in industry. In 1920 the average use was only approximately 115 gallons per day per capita; a 30 percent increase had taken place in 40 years.

Though many industries buy water from the public or municipal supply system, it is common for large factories to put in their own wells or surface reservoirs. The latter type of industrial use may be classed as self-supplied. Statistics on amounts of water for municipal use include the amount of water purchased by some industries.

Annual use

Annual water use in the United States is summarized in Table 9. Use of water to drive generators for electric power development is not included in the table because water is not drawn out of the river for this use but merely routed through the turbines of the power plant.

The total water-use figure, 240,000 million gallons per day, amounts to approximately one-fifth of the amount mentioned at the beginning of this chapter as being available for use. It can be said, then, that at present Americans are using only 1 gallon

Table 9
Annual use of water in the United States, excluding water power

USE	TOTAL WATER WITHDRAWN (MILLION GALLONS PER DAY)		PERCENT
Public supplies	17,000		7
Rural use	3,000		1
Irrigation:			
Delivered to farms 81,000		34	
Lost from canals 29,000		12	
Total irrigation	110,000		46
Self-supplied industrial	110,000		46
Total	240,000		100

out of every 5 available. Of each gallon now being used, only 7 percent is used for public water supplies. The remaining percentage is divided equally between irrigation and industry. These figures indicate that there is no overall shortage of water in the United States.

However, an adequate water supply does not prevent the occurrence of local shortages and excesses, which result from the irregular distribution of precipitation, the arid Southwest, the humid East, and the very rainy mountains of the Northwest. Similar types of problems arise from the season-to-season and year-to-year variation of precipitation in any given area and from the chance occurrence of series of dry years.

Some of these facts can be summarized in diagrammatic form. Figure 42 shows the division of water withdrawn or used for public and industrial uses and for irrigation use in the United States. The part of each that is lost by consumptive use is indicated in the diagrams.

Figure 43 shows the source of water used. Most of it is withdrawn from lakes and streams; 20 percent is withdrawn from

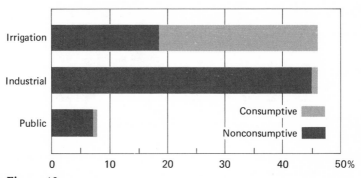

Figure 42
Water use in the United States. Of the 46 percent used for irrigation, 60 percent is consumptively used or becomes vapor. Neither industrial nor public use results in such large consumptive losses. (U.S.G.S.)

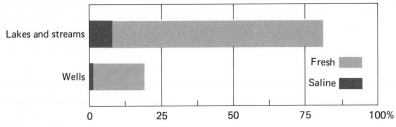

Figure 43
Source and character of water withdrawn for all uses. Eighty percent of the
water used is from lakes and streams and 20 percent is from ground water.
(U.S.G.S.)

ground water. Saline water represents approximately 10 percent
of the water used; all the rest is fresh water.

Figure 44 indicates the material taken in and exported from a
city of 1 million persons. The figures are given in units of tons
per day. It can be seen that the largest item of both import and
export is water: The import is in the form of fresh water for city
uses, and the export is in the form of sewage. Food brought into
the city is only 1/3 of 1 percent of the tonnage represented by
water. More coal than food is brought in per day. Other than
water as sewage, the largest item of export from the city is
refuse, and the second largest is carbon monoxide. Most of the
latter is carried away in the atmosphere.

CITY WATER SYSTEMS

Water purification and distribution

The public is so accustomed to the availability of pure water
at the turn of a tap that no serious consideration has ever been
given to what would be done if the water supply were discon-
tinued for any length of time. Dependability of both supply and
purity is the aim of public water-supply organizations. It is a
tribute to engineers that 17,000 towns and cities and 115 million
persons are served by municipal water systems in the United
States.

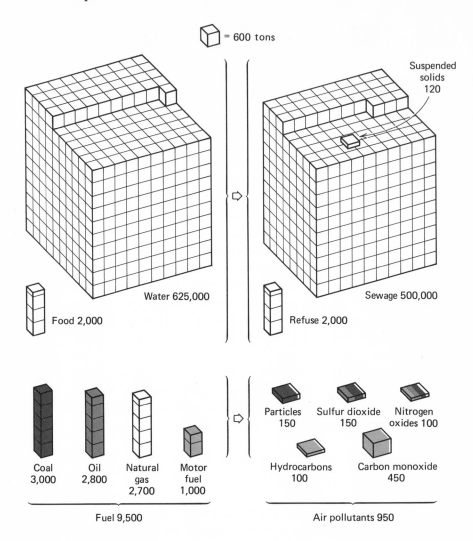

= 600 tons

Suspended solids 120

Water 625,000

Food 2,000

Sewage 500,000

Refuse 2,000

Particles 150   Sulfur dioxide 150   Nitrogen oxides 100

Hydrocarbons 100   Carbon monoxide 450

Coal 3,000   Oil 2,800   Natural gas 2,700   Motor fuel 1,000

Fuel 9,500

Air pollutants 950

Figure 44
Input and outflow from a modern city of 1 million persons. The flow of
materials is expressed as tons per day. Diagram on left shows input; water,
at the rate of 625,000 tons per day, constitutes the major item. The
outflow is dominated by sewage, 500,000 tons per day. (From "Metabolism
of Cities," by Wolman. Copyright © 1965 by Scientific American, Inc.
All rights reserved.)

To appreciate the problems of the design and construction of water-supply systems, it is necessary to be acquainted with the several purposes a water supply must serve. Municipal water systems must be designed to serve much larger demands than merely the average home use of 70 gallons per day per person. They must provide a constant supply for fighting fires and must also meet the demands of industries that buy water from them. These uses increase the daily per capita consumption to more than twice the 70 gallons used in the home.

The need for large amounts of water on demand to fight fires is an important determinant of the sizes of pipes required in a distribution system. The pipes must be able to supply the normal peak demand, which is in summer in the morning or evening, and in addition must be able to supply the fire demand if it coincides with the normal peak demand. Therefore, the size of pipes and the water pressure must be chosen to meet extreme conditions of flow for short periods. However, storage or volume requirements are dictated by the demand during extended periods of heavy water use, which usually occur during a dry period in midsummer.

Approximately 75 percent of American cities derive water from wells; that is, they use ground rather than surface sources. Most municipal wells are pumped with electric power. The modern pump is lowered into the well and placed near the bottom. It creates a pressure that forces the water upward to the surface. Most wells are pumped into a storage reservoir rather than directly into the distribution pipes.

Surface sources usually consist of a stream blocked by a dam that diverts water into pipes or into an aqueduct leading to a storage reservoir. Often the dam itself is high enough to provide storage in the reservoir behind it.

Some storage is always required during periods when demand exceeds average rate of supply. Storage usually serves the additional purpose of providing necessary pressure for water distribution in the pipes. For example, a city reservoir may be located at sufficiently high elevation to provide pressure, or a water tower can be constructed that provides some storage as well as a constant pressure. Pumps are usually required to fill the storage reservoir or water tower. Once the water is up in the tower or reservoir, gravity will distribute the water through the pipes.

Very few cities have such nearly pure water available at the source that no treatment is necessary. In areas where water comes from deep wells or from a fenced and carefully protected watershed, only a minimum of treatment is necessary. This usually consists merely of chlorination; that is, the injection of small amounts of liquid chlorine or other disinfectant into the water to destroy bacteria.

Water commonly has some objectionable odor, taste, or murkiness. Odor and taste can usually be improved by aeration (spraying or trickling the water in such a way that it will be mixed with oxygen in the air). Aeration is the basis for the old saying that water flowing in a stream purifies itself. Given sufficient time and under proper conditions, water usually has enough oxygen dissolved in it already to oxidize organic material. Aeration will tend to improve odor and taste but will not necessarily kill germs; so that old saying should not be considered a truthful one.

Odor, taste, and murkiness are generally improved by the processes of settling and filtering. To settle the impurities, water is run into a large tank where there is but little current and the water is quite still. A finely divided powder, alum, is introduced. The alum forms a "flock," or gelatinlike glob. Thousands of these little masses gradually settle to the bottom of the tank. Impurities stick to the gelatin and are swept out as the floc settles. Just as snowflakes float down through the air, gathering dust and impurities and carrying them to the ground, so does the alum settle out, carrying with it the solid impurities of the water and even bacteria.

The other common treatment is filtering water through a bed of sand. The sand screens out impurities like the filter paper or cloth in a vacuum coffeemaker.

Aeration is sometimes done by spraying water into the air but more often by letting water trickle through a bed of gravel.

Many municipal water-treatment plants use all four methods mentioned, first settling with alum, then filtering through sand, mixing with air, and finally treating by addition of chlorine.

Water-treatment plants reduce the bacterial content of water, improve its taste and odor, and make it clear. Each of these characteristics is constantly being tested in a water-treatment plant and definite standards are required to protect the public health and to assure acceptable quality.

However, salts dissolved in water are not affected by the ordinary treatment measures. In areas where water is in short supply it may be used more than once. Then dissolved salts tend to become more concentrated with each reuse.

Detergents, like the dissolved salts, are not taken out in the water-treatment process. During a recent drought, water from a certain river was used by one city and then discharged back to the river. Cities further downstream used that same water again in turn. The detergents became so concentrated that at times the tap water in cities downstream made suds or bubbles as it emerged from the faucet.

As this incident demonstrates, many cities now are using water that has been discharged through the sewers of cities upstream. Modern water-treatment plants are quite capable of cleaning sewage wastes out of water and making it perfectly safe to drink. People do not like to think they are drinking such purified water, but in fact many are now doing so, and in perfect safety. The public should get used to the fact that water in many places is in such demand that it must be used more than once. This will be done in more areas as the population of the United States grows.

In most cities water is distributed through pipes made of cast iron. Pipes are large near the central water works and become progressively smaller as the system is subdivided. The smallest pipes are those serving houses on an individual street.

The pipes leading from the water main in the street to an individual house are made of galvanized iron or copper. Street mains are generally of 4 or 6 inches in diameter. Such a size not only can carry water to all the houses but can also provide water to fire hydrants when necessary. The pipe leading to most houses is 1 inch in diameter, or occasionally 3/4 inch.

Pressure is required to provide a usable stream of water out of a faucet. The usual pressure in the system of each house is 60 to 70 pounds per square inch. This high pressure is the reason that the water faucet cannot be shut off with the touch of a finger.

How sewage and wastes are treated

Most of the water used in homes is for carrying off wastes. Less water is used for drinking, cooking, and even watering lawns than is used for washing clothes, doing dishes, bathing, flushing the toilet, and operating the sink garbage-disposal unit. Factories use water to dispose of such industrial wastes as chemicals or grease and to carry away excess heat. The cooling of steel and the condensing of steam are examples.

The three types of wastes are animal, vegetable, and mineral. Nearly all domestic or home wastes are animal or vegetable because they are derived from living matter. Detergents and many industrial wastes are mineral in origin. Animal or vegetable matter decays when it is dead and, in so doing, provides food for microscopic bacterial life, which, in turn becomes food for higher organisms and so on through the food chain of living things. Wastes are offensive to sight and smell as well as dangerous to health because they provide food for harmful bacteria that can infect water supplies.

The waste water from homes and factories is carried in the sewer system. This water flows in pipes that, unlike those in the water-supply system, are not under pressure. The slope of the pipe allows gravity to carry the sewage downhill. The sewer network resembles a network of stream channels. The sewer pipes

increase in size as more pipes join together, just as a river increases in size downstream. The pipe under a residential street
in the upper part of the system may be only 6 inches in diameter,
whereas the trunk sewer in a large city may measure several feet.

In the older cities the sewer system carries not only the sanitary sewage—that is, the waste from homes and factories—but
also the storm water from the streets. Treatment plants thus have
to handle a large amount of water during storm periods. In such
circumstances, the bulk of the water is usually diverted so that it
bypasses the treatment plant and flows directly to a river without
treatment. More modern sewerage systems carry the sanitary
wastes in separate pipes from the storm runoff; thus there are
storm sewers and sanitary sewers.

Oxygen is the key element in the satisfactory decomposition
and eventual purification of sewage. The work of oxygen in water
is similar to its work in the body. Oxygen combines with substances that are comparable to fuel; oxidation thus is a burning
process. The oxidation of sewage is not a direct chemical burning,
however. Living organisms consume or burn the organic material of the sewage. The final result is the same as direct oxidation since the end products are stable compounds of oxygen, such
as carbon dioxide and compounds of nitrogen and oxygen
called nitrates.

If raw sewage is dumped into a clean swift stream, the oxygen
in the water that was absorbed from the air and given off by
aquatic plants will begin to decompose the sewage. But the
process uses the dissolved oxygen upon which the fish and the
cleanliness of the stream depend. If the sewage load is small in
relation to the size of the stream, the oxidation can be com-
pleted, and the stream again restores its depleted oxygen from
the air or from plants. But if the oxygen needed to decompose
the sewage exceeds that in the stream, the sewage putrifies. Decay
in the absence of air or oxygen leads to foul-smelling gases. The
carbon and nitrogen of the sewage, instead of being linked to
oxygen, combine with hydrogen and give off such gases as
methane, which is the smell of the marsh, and ammonia. The

sulfur in sewage forms another gas, which is the same gas that gives the odor to spoiled eggs.

Disposing of sewage by dumping it into a stream can be satisfactory, therefore, only when the stream is not overloaded. Because streamflow fluctuates greatly, there is a large variation in the amount of sewage a stream can oxidize satisfactorily. Partly for this reason, sewage loads tend to exceed the natural capacity of rivers to oxidize the wastes. This is one reason that sewage treatment is necessary.

There are various degrees of sewage treatment. In *primary treatment* the sewage first passes through a screen that removes such large objects as sticks and rags. The water then flows slowly through a grit chamber, where sand and silt settle out, and into a large settling tank, where finer suspended solids settle to the bottom or rise to the top. After the material is removed by settling, the water is chlorinated to kill bacteria and is discharged to the stream.

Primary treatment reduces the pollution load of sewage by approximately 35 percent. If greater reduction is required to avoid overloading the stream, then the sewage matter must be oxidized. This is called *secondary treatment.* In one method of secondary treatment, the sewage is slowly sprayed on a bed of coarse stones, usually 6 feet deep. The biological growths that develop on the stones catch the sewage matter and oxidize it. In another method, the sewage is inoculated with microbes that can oxidize organic material. The sewage is then passed into large tanks where it remains long enough for the microbes to break down the organic wastes.

According to the United States Public Health Service, 92 million people in the United States are served by sewer systems. Of these, only 54 million are also provided with sewage treatment. It can be seen from these figures that the waste from a very large population is dumped untreated into rivers.

Many homes that are not connected to sewer systems dispose of their waste water through septic tanks, which are usually underground steel or concrete boxes that are made large enough to hold the water that the household will use during 1 or 2 days. The solids in suspension settle out and the organic matter decomposes in the absence of oxygen. The resulting outflow is offensive to sight and smell but is carried to porous tile drains from which it seeps into the ground.

Troubles arise when accumulated sludge or scum that has floated to the top of the box is not removed. Such accumulations tend to plug up the pores in the soil and the foul-smelling waste then finds its way to the soil surface. If property lots are small and septic tanks of adjoining houses are too close together, there may be insufficient ground area to absorb the water. This condition has been a source of trouble in many suburban housing developments.

IRRIGATION

Plants, like people, need a regular supply of water. Of course, some plants require much more water than others. Many of the grasses and some of the cereals, including wheat and barley, do not use so much as alfalfa, for example. Because the plants that are the most important sources of food and fiber need relatively large amounts of water, most of the farming in the United States is done in areas having at least 20 to 30 inches of precipitation a year.

If crops are to be grown in areas that do not receive enough rainfall during the growing season, the land must be supplied with extra water. Some places have more than enough rainfall in a year to grow any crop, but the rains are inadequate during the growing season. The result is short-term droughts, and during such periods many farmers find it profitable to irrigate their high-priced crops to maintain a high yield and/or a high quality of product.

There are approximately 30 million acres of irrigated land in the United States. Most of it lies in the 17 western states. In 1950 less than 2 million acres of land were being irrigated in the remaining states. More than 1/4 of the entire irrigated area is in

California, more than 1/8 is in Texas, and approximately 1/10 each is in Colorado and Idaho.

In the more humid parts of the United States, irrigation has been increasing rapidly since the 1950's. In the eastern states irrigated acreage has been doubling every 5 years since 1950. Though the bulk of the irrigated land occupies only a portion of the drier parts of the country, approximately 46 percent of all the water used in the United States is used for irrigation.

Irrigation is a consumptive use; that is, most of the water is transpired or evaporated to the atmosphere and is lost to further use by man. Irrigation accounts for the largest portion of the water removed from the stream systems but not returned.

Irrigation demands are large, as are the measurements needed to describe them. Acre-feet are used, rather than gallons. An acre-foot is the quantity of water that will cover 1 acre 1 foot deep and is equivalent to 326,000 gallons. A stream of water delivering 1 cubic foot per second, or $7\frac{1}{2}$ gallons per second, will yield 2 acre-feet in a day's time.

The amount of water required to raise a crop depends on the kind of crop and the climate. The most important climatic characteristic governing water need is the length of the growing season. Since growing seasons are longer in the southern United States, the water required for crops increases further south. Because the growing season is shorter in the cool mountains than in the warmer plains, water requirements decrease at higher elevations.

The following examples give an idea of the amount of water necessary to grow some of the common crops. The quantities are expressed in inches of water necessary to grow the crop in an area where the growing season is approximately 200 days, the average for places where irrigation is widely practiced. Alfalfa requires approximately 35 inches of water; sugar beets need 30 inches; cotton, 25 inches; and potatoes, 20 inches. The water requirement can be supplied by rain during the growing season or by irrigation when adequate water is not supplied by rainfall.

If it were economical to carry water from the natural stream to the field without any waste, irrigation would take much less water than it actually does, for considerable waste results from transporting it. Many irrigation canals and ditches through which the water flows are not lined with concrete or other water-tight material but are merely excavated in the earth. Water flowing in such a ditch tends to seep into the ground, and thus a considerable amount is lost on its way to the farm. Some excess water leaves the irrigated field, so the growing crop does not get to use all the water that the farmer applies to the field. The loss usually is 35 to 50 percent of the total taken out of the stream.

However, not all of the water lost from the ditches or wasted on the field is completely unavailable for man's use. Much of the water that seeps into the ground moves toward a stream channel and reappears as water flowing in a river. In addition, some of the water that flows off the irrigated field is picked up by a drainage ditch and eventually is returned to some surface stream, where it is again available for possible use.

As a consequence of these losses, much more water must be taken from the stream than the previously mentioned figures would indicate. The amounts of water used in irrigation are very large, but it must be remembered that irrigation is the lifestream of many western communities.

As an example of the amount of water used in irrigation, a group of irrigated farms served by a single main canal in southern Arizona might include 20,000 acres of irrigated land. This project would require approximately 110,000 acre-feet of water per year, which is equivalent to 100 million gallons per day or a total of 36 billion gallons per year. Of this amount, 24 billion gallons would be transpired by plants to the atmosphere and would thus be lost to further use by man. Such an amount would support a city of approximately 500,000 people. The remaining 12 billion gallons "wasted" in transporting the water is still part of the regional resource because much of the "waste" returns to the stream from which it was diverted.

Irrigation is more complex than it might appear at first glance. Applying water to the land is an art, and experience is necessary to do the job well. If too little water is applied to a field, the dissolved salts accumulate in the soil just as white lime accumulates in a tea kettle as water continually boils away.

If enough water is applied to the field so that a considerable amount sinks into the soil in excess of that needed by plants, this excess water tends to carry the salts down to the water table where they are beyond the reach of plant roots. Accumulation of salts in the soil is undesirable, as mentioned previously, because in excess they tend to make the soil sticky when wet and to become hard and cloddy when dry. But a means of disposal of this surplus soil water is necessary whether it be used for leaching salts or not. Otherwise this water, added to the ground water, raises the water table. If drainage is not provided, the land will become waterlogged. Practically all irrigated areas have drainage problems.

For two reasons, salt leaching and drainage, the amount of water applied to the field must be carefully chosen. The rate at which the water is applied is also important. If water is applied too fast, the soil cannot absorb the water; consequently, much runs off the surface and is wasted.

Fields that were not adequately smoothed collect too much water in the low spots and are insufficiently watered on the mounds. To achieve uniform crops over the whole field requires careful soil preparation. Some of this difficulty is avoided with the recently developed system of sprinkler irrigation, which results in improved water distribution.

Sprinkler irrigation can now be used even on large fields by using immense sprinkler heads and lightweight, mobile metal pipes. In Hawaii, some sugar-cane fields are sprinkled from large nozzles mounted on permanent standpipes; the main distributing pipes are buried underground, out of the reach of plows and tillage equipment. Obviously, these sprinkler systems are much more expensive than the older and more universal system of furrow or flooding irrigation from an open ditch. The expense of sprinkling systems can be justified only when high-priced crops, which yield a considerable profit from each acre of irrigated land, are being grown.

It can be seen, then, that farming under irrigation is more than merely applying water to compensate for a deficiency in rainfall. The farmer who irrigates must not only pay for the cost of his irrigation system and the extra labor necessary to operate it, but he must also fertilize and spray properly—expensive operations that are profitable only when there is a generous yield of high-priced crops. Irrigation farming therefore requires more time and effort of farm management than does ordinary farming. Not every farmer has the money to start an irrigated farm, the training to operate it, or the desire to expend the necessary effort to succeed.

FARM PONDS

Farm ponds can be seen dotting the landscape of almost every area of the United States. Eastern farmers build ponds for livestock, for raising fish, for a source of water in the event of fire, or for swimming and skating. The western rancher, who is likely to call his pond a "tank" or a "charco," builds ponds almost exclusively for watering livestock.

A farm pond catches and holds water. A small pond is basically like a big reservoir that supplies water to a city or a large irrigated tract. Anyone who builds a farm pond utilizes the same hydrologic principles that the engineer does who builds a reservoir for a big city. There are only approximately 1,250 large reservoirs in the United States; there are millions of farm ponds. Farm ponds are of some importance because they are so numerous.

To be successful, a pond must be large enough for the normal sequence of storms of the region to keep it filled; yet it should not drain so large an area that major floods will wash away the earth fill of the dam. The most common type of farm pond is made by damming a little tributary valley that drains a small watershed in which water flows only when there is a heavy rainstorm. Individually built farm ponds are of great variety; many show much ingenuity in design and construction. Too large a pond means wasted money and maybe wasted water. A pond that is small means water shortage and maybe a washout. Most of the millions of ponds have water surfaces of approximately 1/4 an acre to 2 acres and maximum depths that range from 8 to 15 feet.

Ponds built for irrigation are necessarily larger. A pond of ordinary size contains, when full, enough water for supplementary irrigation for only 8 acres of crops. Nevertheless, in the humid parts of the United States, strategically placed farm ponds might serve to tide crops over short summer dry spells. In the arid regions where irrigation is required during a full growing season and more water is needed for each acre, the reservoir should be large enough to store an amount of water that would average 3 feet in depth over each acre to be irrigated. Reservoirs of such size are large and are no longer "ponds."

Ponds are measured in acres, meaning the surface area when the reservoir is full. The volume of stored water is measured in acre-feet rather than the more familiar unit of gallons because the numbers are more convenient. The volume of a farm pond in acre-feet can be roughly estimated by multiplying the surface area in acres by 40 percent of the maximum depth measured in feet.

Many successful ponds depend entirely on surface runoff from storm rainfall. There must be a watershed of sufficient size draining into the pond to provide enough water to fill it. The water supply will be more assured if the drainage basin is mostly pastured, rather than tilled. A good grass sod does not erode easily and helps keep the inflow relatively clear.

The United States is immense and varied. The amount of runoff an acre of land will yield depends on the climate, soil, and vegetation. For example, in the humid climate of the East, for each acre of watershed the yearly flow of water might be 1/3 or 1/2 an acre-foot. Only 2 or 3 acres of watershed would suffice for each acre-foot of pond. In the desert an acre of watershed might yield only one hundredth of an acre-foot of water; thus 100 acres of watershed would be needed for each acre-foot of pond.

A careful pond builder tests the prospective site by making a few borings with a soil augur or post-hole digger to be sure that the soil is tight enough to hold water. Sandy sites are avoided, clay is best, but any good loam is suitable. A new pond leaks, but deposition of silt tends to decrease the seepage. Even in old ponds, however, seepage is usually greater than loss from evaporation.

Any impoundment of water, whether natural (as a lake) or artificial (as a farm pond), begins to die as soon as it is created. Sediment enters the lake with the water, and most of its stays there. How long a farm pond will be useful depends entirely on how much sediment the tributary catchment delivers to it each year. Ponds have been built that were filled to the brink with sediment in the first year, or by the first flood. Others, of course, provide useful service for many years, but to avoid trouble the careful pond builder considers prospective sedimentation when he builds his farm pond.

A dam built across a draw needs a spillway or a place for flood water to overflow without washing out the dam. The spillway may be an overflow pipe or a piece of firm sodded ground at one end of the dam.

Pond owners are likely to encounter trouble when they neglect some important hydrologic principle. A deep pond holds water longer than a shallow one of the same volume. A pond that is too small for the watershed area will overflow frequently and may wash out. A pond that is too large for the watershed wastes money and water. A dam without an adequate spillway will wash out.

What are some of the benefits of extensive building of farm ponds? They trap a good deal of storm runoff, several millions of acre-feet a year. This water is available for watering stock, for raising fish, for recreation, or just to look at. Considerable sediment is also trapped. Ponds may add some water to ground storage but the amount has not been evaluated.

What are the costs? There is a loss of water by evaporation, a loss that is more important in the arid West than in the humid East but one that is still significant during summer droughts. A reservoir might be thought to salvage the water that would be lost, but a farmer, a power plant, a factory, or a city may be counting on the water that would have passed on downstream in the absence of the reservoir. The problem of ponds may be critical because the water in ranch ponds is mostly lost to the atmosphere rather than used. A beef cow needs only 10 gallons of water per day, and 100 head of cattle need only half an acre-foot per season. Capacity in excess is not used and is subject to loss by evaporation and seepage.

The amount of loss can be minimized by making the pond deep and small in area. Since these proportions rarely exist at natural dam sites, a water-conserving pond can be built by excavating a deep pit with narrow sloping sides. An economical stock pond would be small in capacity, say, 1/2 an acre-foot, but of great depth, 10 or 15 feet. In a tight soil, this kind of reservoir is not only droughtproof but water conserving. A poorly designed pond is not only an uncertain water supply but wastes water that others downstream could put to use.

The water caught in farm ponds cannot contribute greatly to flood control, for farm ponds intercept the flow from only a relatively small part of the watershed area. In addition, a farm pond is kept full and has little space for storing flood water, and when a pond is low after a drought, the soil is also dry and floods are not likely to occur.

For these reasons, it should be recognized that a farm pond is a form of water use or depletion. Properly built, it can use water efficiently.

FLOOD CONTROL

An understanding of how flood plains are formed (see p. 83) should make it obvious that a river channel is not large enough to contain all the water produced by a drainage basin in times of heavy precipitation. To flood (that is, to discharge in excess of channel capacity) is a natural characteristic of rivers. Thus the flood plain is a normal part of the river during times of exceptional discharge.

Flood plains are particularly valuable to man because their soils are generally fertile and because such areas are flat and easy to use. For example, the flat terrain makes the flood plain a good place to build railroad lines, highways, warehouses, and storage areas. Proximity to a river is often convenient if boats or barges are used for transport.

If there were not some particular advantage, it would seem foolish indeed for people to establish communities on flood plains. Generally they do because they do not know better. Then one day the river floods, and most people who are in the way of the river suddenly wish they lived or worked up on a hill. But by that time it is too late. They own a house or other property on the flood plain and cannot afford to move. Therefore, people whose work makes it particularly advantageous to be on a flood plain should realize that these advantages are obtained at the risk of flood damage.

Because the aim of flood control is the reduction of flood damage, this end can also be achieved by informing people of the dangers and encouraging those who gain no advantage from living on the flood plain not to build there. Maps can be drawn to show areas subject to flooding and the relative frequency of flooding. Such information could be made the basis for protective regulations. For example, most cities have a rule that residences may be built no closer to the street than, say, 25 feet. Also, houses must be at least a specified number of feet from a property line. In business districts other rules apply. Hydrologic principles lend logical support to the idea of similar zoning rules to restrict the use of flood plains. Such zoning regulations could be an effective way of reducing flood damage. This method has not been generally used, but it appears to be gaining recognition.

The much more common method of reducing flood damage is to keep the water from overflowing the flood plain where factories, homes, or other valuable properties have been built, by walling the water off; that is, by constructing levees or dikes along the river banks. A second way is to store the flood water in a reservoir behind a dam and release it at such a slow rate that the river downstream does not overflow. These two principal methods rely on engineering works and are relatively expensive.

Though simple in principle, reservoirs are complex devices. For example, construction of a series of small dams on upstream tributaries is often considered as a solution to the flood-control problem. Because this example brings out several important hydrologic principles, it is instructive to compare the effects of a series of small dams with those of a single larger dam on the main river. The comparison shows that large dams and small dams serve different purposes and that one type cannot substitute for the other.

The human hand can be viewed as an example of the way in which a natural drainage basin is constructed. The four fingers and thumb might be likened to the tributaries to the main river, represented by the forearm at the wrist. The fingers and thumb do not make up the whole. If the flow of blood were stopped by application of pressure at the base of each finger and the thumb, the flow of blood through the wrist would not be completely stopped because there is the area of the palm that contributes blood to the veins passing through the wrist. However, if pressure were applied at the wrist, then the flow of blood through the whole hand would be stopped.

The tributaries of a river added together do not constitute the whole of a river basin drainage network, just as the arteries and veins in the fingers and thumb do not constitute the entire system of blood vessels in the hand. There is a land area that drains directly to the main river and that is not included in the drainage of any of the individual tributaries.

The sum of the areas of all the tributary basins in a drainage area is approximately half the total area; that is, in most drainage basins, the larger tributaries drain, on the average, approximately half the total area of the basin. Consequently, if flood-control dams were built at the mouth of each tributary, they would catch flood water from only half the basin area; but a dam constructed on the main river at its mouth would control run-off from the entire basin.

If flood-producing rainfall fell only on the uppermost tributaries, flooding would occur only a moderate distance down the main channel even if no dams existed on the upper tributaries, because the main channel naturally gets larger downstream. At some point, therefore, the channel gets large enough to contain all the flood water produced by the upstream tributaries even if there are no dams on them.

Such land-management measures as contour plowing, terracing, and strip-cropping are not effective in reducing major floods. The main effect of these practices is to increase the amount of water infiltrated into the soil. As previously mentioned, major floods occur only when previous rain or snowmelt has almost saturated the soil. These practices are more or less effective in minimizing soil erosion and increasing crop production.

Flooding causes great damage to agricultural land bordering small headwater tributaries. This damage results more from frequent small floods than from a few major ones. Construction of small headwater dams is effective protection against these frequent overflows in tributary valleys but the great floods, such as those in Connecticut in 1954, on the Mississippi River in 1927, and on the Kansas River in 1951, cannot be effectively controlled even by a myraid of small headwater dams.

Thus it can be seen that to control the major or catastrophic floods, large dams on the main streams, in combination with levees, are the only effective engineering works. These barriers, however, since they are on the main channels, are downstream from the many minor valleys that also experience flood damage. Thus upstream dams are needed for control of damage there. Large and small dams clearly serve different purposes.

In 1960, the federal government had spent approximately $4 billion in the construction of flood-control works, and most of this has been spent since 1936. More than 300 separate projects have been completed, most of them large dams. Nearly twice as many are already planned but not yet started. Flood control by engineering works has been expensive and will be even more so in the future. However, these projects have prevented much flood damage that would have occurred if the projects had not been built. The completed flood-control projects prevent approximately $300 million of flood damage every year. Nevertheless, flood damage continues to grow. Flood damage in the United States has shown no tendency to decrease since 1936 when the national flood-control program began. While flood-control engineers grimly strive to abate the flood toll by constructing reservoirs and levees, cities and factories inexorably invade the flood plains. The damage caused by floods increases each year.

Who pays the bill for these flood-control expenditures? The people whose lands or property are situated where floods can damage them carry only a small part of the cost of the dams or other engineering works that are built to protect them. The federal law allows approximately 90 percent of the total cost of the flood-control works to be paid for out of the federal treasury. All citizens, through their taxes, share in carrying the cost of flood-control works.

With the growing population and expanding cities, the most effective flood protection method is to keep the flood plains as free as possible of new homes, factories, and other damageable property.

WATER POWER

Water was one of the first sources of power, other than the muscle of man or beast, for doing useful work. The old-time mill put water to work for grinding grain or sawing logs by directing a flow over one side of a wooden wheel, the rim of which was lined with buckets. The wheel turned because it was loaded on one side by the flowing water caught in the buckets. These old water wheels were awkward and cumbersome and could not supply large amounts of power. The modern reaction turbine was developed approximately 100 years ago when power for factories became the need.

In the turbine, water flows down from a "head race" through curved vanes. The water pushes against the vanes and turns them. In high-speed turbines the vanes act like the propeller of a ship.

Until the development of electrical power, factories like the gristmill were built along streams. A small dam was built to create a "fall" to operate the turbine that was used to run the machinery. Lowell, Massachusetts, and Paterson, New Jersey, were originally hydraulic towns (that is, towns that depended on water power). In such towns water diverted from the rivers was often carried in tiers of canals. Factories took water from one canal and discharged it into the next lower one. After electrical power became a reality, it was more efficient to generate electrical power and to carry the power to the factory by wires.

Approximately 20 percent of all electrical power used in the United States today is generated by water power. In 1940, approximately 40 percent was produced by water power. Although the amount produced by water power, as measured in kilowatts, has increased threefold in the past 25 years, the total amount of electricity produced has increased sixfold. Most of the increased demand for power has been met by generating plants that burn coal, gas, or oil. Why is water power becoming the source of relatively less and less of the total electric power? Any why is this trend likely to continue?

Any river can produce power, but only at a few places can power be produced economically. These places are on the larger rivers where slope is great, where the flow is large and steady, and where the valley is narrow enough to make a good site for a dam. Most power sites that meet these requirements have been recognized and their potential has been appraised. There is a simple formula for calculating power: Multiply the fall in feet by the rate of flow in cubic feet per second, divide the product by 11, and the result is horsepower. For example, the fall at Hoover Dam is 530 feet, the flow averages approximately 18,000 cubic feet per second, and the output should be 870,000 horsepower. This is close to the actual power, 800,000 horsepower, developed at Hoover Dam.

Waterpower is free in the sense that no fuel is used to produce it. Moreover, it does not directly consume water. From a conservation point of view, therefore, waterpower may be considered advantageous, but the development of waterpower uses materials. In the American economy the cost of the materials, with their incident cost for labor, needed in most places to produce waterpower is greater than the cost of producing electricity by fuel power.

There is another consideration. Fuel power and atomic power can be made available whenever power is wanted. Because river flow is variable, a waterpower plant may be able to yield only a fraction of its potential capacity on demand. Undependable power is less valuable than "firm power." For this reason, reservoir storage is built to store water during periods of high flow for use when the flow is low, in an effort to "firm up" the power supply. Storage costs not only money but water in the form of evaporation.

The average vertical distance traversed by water in rivers of the United States is approximately 1,650 feet. These falling waters, whose average flow is approximately 2,000,000 cubic feet per second, represent 300 million horsepower, an enormous amount that is greater than that required by all present needs.

Of the 300 million horsepower represented by the flow of water downstream to the sea, engineers estimate that only approximately 100 million horsepower can be generated at practical power sites. Of this potential only 38 million horsepower has been developed—25 million of this since 1930. A considerable part of this 25 million horsepower is a byproduct of major reservoirs built by the federal government for flood control and irrigation. Water released from these reservoirs can be passed through turbines to generate electric power. Production of electricity by waterpower will probably double or triple in the last quarter of the twentieth century, and a good part of it will come from reservoirs built for the multiple purposes of flood control, irrigation, recreation, and power. However, in relation to total electric power production, production by waterpower is likely to continue to decrease. At present less than 2 percent of the power used in the United States comes from nuclear reactors. It is difficult to speculate about the amount of electric power that may, in the next quarter century, have a nuclear source.

FACTS ABOUT WATER

This primer has attempted to show that ground water is understandable. It is not a mystery detectable only by ancient arts or forked sticks. Moreover, locating ground water is only the first step. Further information on recharge rates, the specific yield, and the permeability is required to put ground water to use.

It is common to suppose that the recharge of ground-water reservoirs can be increased by holding the raindrops on the land. It might be assumed that pouring a bucket of water on the absorbent earth increases the ground-water resource by just that amount. This primer has shown why this assumption may be wrong. Soil moisture and evapotranspiration may remove the water long before it can penetrate to the water table.

Water facts can help to avoid glaring mistakes and thus aid efforts toward conservation.

The United States is in the happy circumstance of being well supplied with water. After Nature takes its share of the water that falls as precipitation, there is available for man's use approximately 7,500 gallons of water per day for every citizen. Of this available water, 1 gallon is used out of every 5.

Thus the nation as a whole is not likely to run out of water in the foreseeable future. But because water is not uniformly available in various parts of the United States, it is necessary to bring water from places of excess to places of shortage. Such transport of water, whether in river channels, canals, or pipes, costs money. There is an economic limit, therefore, to the amount of water that can be transported to places where it is in short supply.

In this sense, then, available water is limited principally by how much any area or group can afford to spend to increase its local supply. In areas where water is in short supply, obviously, conservation (minimizing useless waste and applying available water to uses that give the greatest social and economic benefit) is both desirable and necessary.

Every year the United States Geological Survey publishes several score of informative reports concerning the topics described in this primer—rivers, ground water, water chemistry, and water use. Each year it renders an accounting of the flow in the rivers of the United States. Outstanding events like floods and droughts are given special record in these reports. More than 10,000 pages of data are published each year.

Water engineers, water geologists, and water chemists collect and publish these facts for just one purpose: to make it possible to manage the nation's water resources in accord with the realities of Nature. These facts are available to everyone.

Flood control, irrigation, water supply, and pollution control are examples of water projects whose merits are hammered out in public discussion. Hydrologic principles are not controversial. The more that is known about hydrology, the easier it is to judge alternate proposals and to compare their benefits. The better informed the citizen, the sounder will be the nation's development of its water resources.

Glossary

Acre-foot. A unit quantity of water; the amount that will cover 1 acre to a depth of 1 foot; consists of 326,000 gallons.

Alum. A chemical substance (usually potassium aluminum sulfate) that is gelatinous when wet; used in water-treatment plants for settling out small particles of foreign matter.

Consumptive use. Use of water resulting in a large proportion of loss to the atmosphere by evapotranspiration. Irrigation is a consumptive use.

Crumb. A unit or particle of soil composed of many small grains sticking together.

Cubic feet per second (cfs). A measure of discharge; the amount of water passing a given point, expressed as number of cubic feet in each second.

Current meter. A device for measuring water velocity, consisting of a propeller that turns at a rate dependent on the water velocity.

Discharge. Outflow; the flow of a stream, canal, or aquifer. It is also common to refer to the discharge of a canal or stream into a lake, river, or an ocean.

Divide, drainage divide (sometimes called *watershed*). The boundary between one drainage basin and another.

Domestic use. Use of water in homes and on lawns, including use for laundry, washing cars, cooling, and swimming pools.

Draw. A tributary valley or coulee that usually discharges water only after a rainstorm.

Ephemeral stream. A natural channel that carries water after a storm but is otherwise dry.

Evaporation. The process by which water is changed from a liquid to a gas or vapor.

Evapotranspiration. Water withdrawn from soil by evaporation and plant transpiration. This water is transmitted to the atmosphere as vapor.

Flood. Any relatively high streamflow overtopping the natural or artificial banks in any reach of a stream.

Flood plain. The lowland that borders a river, usually dry but subject to flooding when the stream overflows its banks. It is that flat area constructed by the present river in the present climate.

Food chain. The dependence of one type of life on another, each in turn eating or absorbing the next organism in the chain. Grass is eaten by cow; cow is eaten by man. This food chain involves grass, cow, man.

Gage height. The elevation of the water surface as measured by a staff marked off in feet and parts of feet.

Gaging station. The installation of a stilling well connected to the river and a float activating a recorder.

Head race. The pipe or chute through which water falls downward into the turbine of a power plant.

Humus. Organic matter in or on a soil; composed of partly or fully decomposed bits of plant tissue derived from plants on or in the soil, or from animal manure.

Hydrograph. A plot of discharge as a function of time.

Hydrology. The science of the behavior of water in the atmosphere, on the earth's surface, and underground.

Infiltration. The flow of a fluid into a substance through pores or small openings. The word is commonly used to denote the flow of water into soil material.

Mean annual flood. The arithmetic mean of the highest peak discharge during each year of record.

Mean annual flow. The average of all the days of record of discharge, expressed as a figure in cubic feet per second. It is the uniform flow, which, if multiplied by the number of seconds in a year, gives the volume of water that passed the point in question in an average year.

Leaching. The removal in solution of the more soluble minerals by percolating waters.

Nonconsumptive use. Uses of water in which only a small part of the water is lost to the atmosphere by evapotranspiration or by combination with a manufactured product. Nonconsumptive uses return to the stream or the ground approximately the same amount as diverted or used.

Permeability. The property of soil or rock that allows passage of water through it. This depends not only on the volume of the openings and pores but also on how these openings are connected to each other.

Rating curve. A plot of discharge as a function of gage height. Data for a rating curve are obtained by current meter measurements of discharge.

Reach. A finite length of river, a few hundred feet or several thousands of feet.

Reaction turbine. A type of water wheel in which water turns the blades of a rotor, which then drives an electrical generator or other machine.

Salts. Dissolved chemical substances in water; table salt (sodium chloride) is but one of many such compounds that are found in water.

Sediment. Fragmental mineral material transported or deposited by water or air.

Self-supplied industrial use. Water supply developed by an individual industry or factory for its own use.

Specific yield. The amount of water that can be obtained from the pores or cracks of a unit volume of soil or rock.

Structure (in soil). Relation of particles or groups of particles that impart to the whole soil a characteristic manner of breaking; some types are crumb structure, block structure, platy structure, columnar structure.

Swale. Draw, coulee, or small valley.

Terrace. A former flood plain no longer being actively constructed by the river in the present climate; an abandoned flood plain.

Transpiration. The process by which water vapor escapes from the living plant and enters the atmosphere.

Watershed or drainage area. An area from which water drains to a single point; in a natural basin, the area contributing flow to a given place or a given point on a stream.

Water table. The top of the zone of saturation in the ground.

Weathering. Decomposition, mechanical and chemical, of rock material under the influence of climatic factors of water, heat, and air.

Equivalents

1 cubic foot per second (cfs) = 450 gallons per minute, or $7\frac{1}{2}$ gallons per second

1 cfs for 1 day, or 1 cfs-day, = approximately 2 acre-feet

1 acre-foot = 326,000 gallons

1 cubic foot weighs 62.4 pounds

1 cubic foot = 7.48 gallons

1 gallon = 8.33 pounds

1 ton = 240 gallons

1 inch per hour from 1 sq mi = 640 cfs

1 cubic meter per second = 35.3 cfs

1 inch per hour from 1 acre = 1 cfs

1 inch = 2.54 cm

1 mile = 1.61 km

1 acre is 208.7 feet on a side

1 km^2 = .386 mi^2

Index